ARLEN AND HARBURG'S
Over the Rainbow

Oxford KEYNOTES

Series Editor KEVIN C. KARNES

Sergei Prokofiev's Alexander Nevsky
KEVIN BARTIG

Rodgers and Hammerstein's Carousel
TIM CARTER

Aaron Copland's Appalachian Spring
ANNEGRET FAUSER

Arvo Pärt's Tabula Rasa
KEVIN C. KARNES

Beethoven's Symphony No. 9
ALEXANDER REHDING

Arlen and Harburg's Over the Rainbow
WALTER FRISCH

Oxford KEYNOTES

ARLEN AND HARBURG'S *Over the Rainbow*

WALTER FRISCH

Oxford University Press is a department of the University of Oxford. It furthers the University's objective of excellence in research, scholarship, and education by publishing worldwide. Oxford is a registered trade mark of Oxford University Press in the UK and certain other countries.

Published in the United States of America by Oxford University Press
198 Madison Avenue, New York, NY 10016, United States of America.

Library of Congress Cataloging-in-Publication Data
Names: Frisch, Walter, 1951–
Title: Arlen and Harburg's Over the rainbow / Walter Frisch.
Description: New York, NY: Oxford University Press, [2017] |
Series: Oxford keynotes | Includes bibliographical references and index.
Identifiers: LCCN 2017008890 | ISBN 9780190467333 (hardcover)
|ISBN 9780190467340 (pbk.)
Subjects: LCSH: Arlen, Harold, 1905–1986. Wizard of Oz. Over the rainbow. |
Harburg, E. Y. (Edgar Yipsel), 1896–1981.
Classification: LCC ML410.A76 F75 2017 | DDC 782.42164—dc23
LC record available at https://lccn.loc.gov/2017008890

Series Editor's INTRODUCTION

OXFORD KEYNOTES REIMAGINES THE canons of Western music for the twenty-first century. With each of its volumes dedicated to a single composition or album, the series provides an informed, critical, and provocative companion to music as artwork and experience. Books in the series explore how works of music have engaged listeners, performers, artists, and others through history and in the present. They illuminate the roles of musicians and musics in shaping Western cultures and societies, and they seek to spark discussion of ongoing transitions in contemporary musical landscapes. Each approaches its key work in a unique way, tailored to the distinct opportunities that the work presents. Targeted at performers, curious listeners, and advanced undergraduates, volumes in the series are written by expert and engaging voices in their fields, and will therefore be of significant interest to scholars and critics as well.

In selecting titles for the series, Oxford Keynotes balances two ways of defining the canons of Western music: as lists of works that critics and scholars deem to have articulated key moments in the history of the art, and as lists of works that comprise the bulk of what consumers listen to, purchase, and perform today. Often, the two lists intersect, but the overlap is imperfect. While not neglecting the first, Oxford Keynotes gives considerable weight to the second. It confronts the musicological canon with the living repertoire of performance and recording in classical, popular, jazz, and other idioms. And it seeks to expand that living repertoire through the latest musicological research.

Kevin C. Karnes
Emory University

CONTENTS

ABOUT THE COMPANION WEBSITE

Oxford University Press has created a website to accompany *Arlen and Harburg's Over the Rainbow* that features a variety of related multimedia materials. Many of these resources are integral to the volume itself or provide needed and useful context. As with all of the websites for Oxford Keynotes volumes, the reader is encouraged to take advantage of this valuable online information to expand their experience beyond the print book in hand. Examples available online are indicated in the text with Oxford's symbol ▶.

www.oup.com/us/ahotr
Username: Music3
Password: Book3234

The reader is invited to explore the full catalog of Oxford Keynotes volumes on the series homepage.
www.oup.com/us/oxfordkeynotes

ACKNOWLEDGMENTS

MANY PEOPLE HAVE BEEN extraordinarily generous with their time, expertise, and materials as I researched and wrote this book. I am especially grateful to Laura Lynn Broadhurst for sharing many primary sources she has uncovered in connection with her PhD dissertation in progress (Rutgers University) on the songs for *The Wizard of Oz,* and to John Fricke, *Oz* and Judy Garland expert extraordinaire, who has also provided me many documents and invaluable advice. I have had many long, fruitful exchanges with both Laura and John. Of course, any errors of fact or differences of interpretation remain my responsibility alone.

Series editor Kevin Karnes has been a supportive and keenly critical reader. Daniel Callahan, Kevin Fellezs, Dee Michel, and Loren Schoenberg kindly read chapters and offered many helpful reactions and suggestions. Daniel Goldmark read the manuscript for Oxford University Press and offered many valuable suggestions. My partner Marilyn McCoy read and commented on a complete draft, as always with sharp insight and deep sympathy. My sons,

Nick and Simon Frisch, contributed thoughts that have been most welcome. Simon prepared the musical examples.

Other individuals who have responded to my queries, on whose knowledge or skills I have relied, or who have been generous in sharing materials, include Rita Arlen, Gilbert Baker, Ken Bloom, George Chauncey, Gregory Chen, Eric Davis, Todd Decker, Michael Feinstein, Michelle Fisher, Will Friedwald, John Haley, Michael Hearn, Aaron Johnson, Miles Kreuger, Robert O'Meally, Nathan Platte, William Rosar, Phil Schaap, Lawrence Schulman, Dariusz Terefenko, Chris Washburne, David Weiner, and Leanne Wood.

I would also like to acknowledge others who have provided access to source materials essential to this project: Mark Eden Horowitz at the Library of Congress, Nick Markovich at the Yip Harburg Foundation, Ned Comstock at the Cinematic Arts Library of the University of Southern California, Kristine Krueger at the Margaret Herrick Library of the Academy of Motion Picture Arts and Sciences, Emily Ferrigno at the Irving S. Gilmore Music Library at Yale University, and Tad Hershorn at the Rutgers Institute of Jazz Studies.

RECORDINGS AND PRIMARY SOURCES

WHERE I REFER TO recordings of "Over the Rainbow," I have included timings to help the reader locate the place in the recording being discussed. Many of the recordings can be heard on the companion website for the book.

Some primary sources consulted for this book are located in the following collections, which will be referenced in abbreviated form in the text:

LC	The Library of Congress (Washington, DC)
YHF	The Yip Harburg Foundation (New York City)
CAL	The Cinematic Arts Library at the University of Southern California (Los Angeles)
MHL	The Margaret Herrick Library of the Academy of Motion Picture Arts and Sciences (Beverly Hills, CA)
LL	The Lilly Library at Indiana University (Bloomington)
IGL	The Irving Gilmore Music Library at Yale University (New Haven, CT)

ARLEN AND HARBURG'S

Over the Rainbow

INTRODUCTION

LESS THAN A YEAR after the release of *The Wizard of Oz* by Metro-Goldwyn-Mayer (MGM) in 1939, its hit song "Over the Rainbow" turned up in another film from the same studio, *The Philadelphia Story*. Katherine Hepburn, playing a wealthy socialite on the eve of her wedding, and James Stewart, a tabloid reporter sent to get a scoop on the event, share a drunken (but innocent) midnight swim at her family estate. As he carries her back to the house, Stewart sings a garbled version of "Over the Rainbow," humming or improvising when he can't recall the lyrics ("*Someday* over the rainbow"). "Don't stop, Mikey," Hepburn murmurs. "Keep crooning." (View example 0.1 ▶.)

At the time of *The Philadelphia Story*, "Over the Rainbow" was a still a new song. Created in the spring of 1938 by composer Harold Arlen and lyricist E. Y. ("Yip") Harburg, it had appeared in the summer of 1939 in the MGM movie musical *The Wizard of Oz*, sung by Judy Garland as the character Dorothy. By including "Over the Rainbow" in *The Philadelphia Story* as a part of the film's narrative, sung by one character to another, MGM was offering a tongue-in-cheek salute to a song they had almost cut from *The Wizard of Oz* because it was felt to slow up the action. Dorothy's wistful ballad, sung in a dusty farmyard, is transformed into a drunken serenade in a sophisticated romantic comedy set on the Main Line. "Over the Rainbow" had traveled far and quickly from the world of the original film. Clearly—to paraphrase one of the most famous lines in movie history—we are not in Kansas anymore.

"Over the Rainbow" followed a number of different paths out of MGM's Kansas. De-sentimentalized in *The Philadelphia Story*, the song would assume a hallowed status in the coming decades. Garland called it "sacred"; Salman Rushdie, a "hymn."[1] The saccharine closing moments of the 1998 film *You've Got Mail* capture something of what the song has conveyed for much of its later history. Kathleen (Meg Ryan) and Joe (Tom Hanks) meet in Riverside Park in New York, and she realizes tearfully that the man she loves and her email pen pal are one and the same. Harry Nilsson's smooth version of "Over the Rainbow" wafts over the soundtrack as Joe tells Kathleen, "Don't cry, Shopgirl." "I wanted it to be you," she sobs. "I wanted it to be you so badly" (view example 0.1 ▶). Here "Over the Rainbow" expresses hope for fulfillment after struggle, or for the triumph of love over strife. *Per aspera ad astra*—through hardships we reach the stars (or go over the rainbow).

"Over the Rainbow" is one of the most beloved songs of all time. In a survey conducted in 2000, the National Endowment for the Arts and the Recording Industry Association of America asked elected officials, people in the music industry and media, and teachers and students what they felt was the greatest song of the twentieth century. "Over the Rainbow" won handily, beating out such titles as "White Christmas," "This Land Is Your Land," and "Respect." In 2004, the American Film Institute put "Over the Rainbow" at the head of a list of the top one hundred songs in American cinema.[2] At the Oscar ceremonies in 2014, to celebrate the seventy-fifth anniversary of the release of *The Wizard of Oz*, the singer Pink performed "Over the Rainbow" before forty-three million television viewers worldwide.

How and why did "Over the Rainbow" accrue its many meanings, as well as its iconic status in American music and in popular culture more broadly? This book attempts to answer those questions through a selective "biography" of the song, from its origins in *The Wizard of Oz*, a rich story on its own, through a good part of eight decades. Like a painting, poem, or novel, a song moves through history attracting new audiences and—in the case of music—performers, who project onto it their values, their concerns. In recent years American popular song has been recognized as a valuable site for exploring such cultural and social connections, as shown in studies of Jerome Kern and Oscar Hammerstein's "Ol' Man River," and Irving Berlin's "Blue Skies," "White Christmas," and "God Bless America."[3] In each case, authors explore how the song transcends its initial identity as a piece of sheet music, a recording, or a number from a show or film. And yet there is also an essence, something of the original work that carries through time.

This book attempts to strike a balance between discovering an essential "Over the Rainbow" and tracing its journey over many generations. Chapter 1 examines the genesis of "Over the Rainbow" from placeholder status as Dorothy's "Kansas" number in screenplay drafts of *The Wizard of Oz* to its fashioning as the ballad we know by Arlen and Harburg. Chapter 2 unfolds the next stages in the history of "Over the Rainbow": the several reprises of "Over the Rainbow" planned for the film but eventually rejected; the consternation of MGM executives when a copy of the song was leaked prematurely to a popular bandleader, who made a recording; the removal of the song during a preview of the film; and finally the radio broadcasts and newly authorized recordings that accompanied the elaborate publicity rollout for *The Wizard of Oz*.

Chapter 3 presents a close reading of the music and lyrics of "Over the Rainbow," an undisputed masterpiece that blends crystalline melodic simplicity and elegant harmonic sophistication within a standard structure of thirty-two bars (plus a coda). "Over the Rainbow" was the signature song of Judy Garland, the subject of chapter 4. After *The Wizard of Oz*, she continued to perform it for thirty years, in concerts and recordings and on radio and television. Emblematic of Garland's personal and professional struggles, "Over the Rainbow" also carried a message of hope to her fans, including gay men during the 1960s and 70s.

"Over the Rainbow" has always been a popular standard among jazz pianists, a realm where there is no direct competition with Garland. Chapter 5 will explore how Art Tatum, Bud Powell, Erroll Garner, Dick Marx, André Previn, and Keith Jarrett work wondrous changes upon Arlen's distinctive melody and richly chromatic harmonic language.

Chapter 6 examines the new life "Over the Rainbow" took on after a version released in 1993 by the Hawaiian pop singer Israel Kamakawiwo'ole featured it in a medley with "What a Wonderful World." Originally reflecting the singer's advocacy for Hawaiian sovereignty at a time when indigenous land rights were under threat, the track soon attained a global following when it appeared on many commercials, films, and television shows.

As I worked on this project, many versions of "Over the Rainbow" came to my attention, including a video in which a man plays the tune by squeezing differently pitched stuffed cats and another in which Dorothy's original scene from *The Wizard of Oz* is given a death metal voice-over.[4] Even in a larger study it would be impossible to explore all the identities, sublime or ridiculous, that "Over the Rainbow" has assumed. More than most numbers in the so-called Great American Songbook—the enduring popular standards created between about 1920 and 1970—"Over the Rainbow" has proved a palimpsest. A palimpsest in its traditional meaning is a manuscript page that has been overwritten many times by successive generations yet on which traces of the original image remain. So it is with "Over the Rainbow." Generations of performers and listeners have read into the song their own concerns and hopes in ways that update but never efface the plight of young Dorothy Gale in Kansas.

CHAPTER 1
CREATING THE RAINBOW

THE PARTNERSHIP BETWEEN COMPOSER Harold Arlen and lyricist E. Y. ("Yip") Harburg, lasting over four decades, was one of the most successful and enduring in the history of American popular song (figure 1.1). Their first collaboration dates from 1932, when Harburg (with Billy Rose) wrote the lyrics to one of Arlen's first big hits, "Paper Moon." They went on to write songs for a number of Hollywood films, including *The Singing Kid* with Al Jolson (1936), and two scores for Broadway, the 1934 revue *Life Begins at 8:40* and the 1937 show *Hooray for What?* Not long after writing music for *The Wizard of Oz* in 1938, Arlen and Harburg would contribute to another MGM film, the Marx Brothers' *At the Circus*, released in October 1939. That

FIGURE 1.1 E. Y. "Yip" Harburg and Harold Arlen in the 1930s. Photo by Adolph Altman for American Society of Composers, Authors and Publishers (ASCAP)

within such a short time span a composer-lyricist team could create a ballad like "Over the Rainbow" for Garland and the brilliant "list" number "Lydia, the Tattooed Lady" for Groucho Marx is a testament to both their enormous range and their artistic compatibility.

In later years, even when Arlen began to work more frequently with other lyricists, he and Harburg continued their partnership, with scores for the shows *Bloomer Girl* (1944) and *Jamaica* (1957) and an animated film with Garland, *Gay Purr-ee* (1962). Two of the last songs Arlen worked on before Parkinson's disease made him unable to compose were also collaborations with Harburg, "Looks Like the End of a Beautiful Friendship" and "Promise Me Not to Love Me," both from 1976.

"In the Shade of the New Apple Tree," an Arlen-Harburg song from the musical *Hooray for What?*, caught the attention of Arthur Freed, an associate producer for *The Wizard of Oz* at MGM and an accomplished lyricist himself. Freed admired the number's jaunty but sophisticated simplicity, its tuneful melody underpinned by chromatically tinged harmonies. These were just the features that Freed desired—and would get—in the songs for *The Wizard of Oz*. Arlen beat out several more senior songwriters for the *Oz* assignment, including Jerome Kern and Nacio Herb Brown (Freed's own collaborator). When Arlen told Kern, a figure revered in Broadway and Hollywood, about being approached by Freed to write the score, the elder composer said to him with incredulity but respect, "You got the job?"[1]

In early May 1938 Arlen and Harburg were given a fourteen-week contract for *The Wizard of Oz*. By the time they came on board, the film had been in development for several months. A number of writers were preparing scenarios or screenplays under the supervision of Freed and executive producer Mervyn LeRoy. Eventually no fewer than fourteen screenwriters, including Harburg, would work on the film.

"Over the Rainbow" is the only musical number to be sung in Kansas and is also by far the most serious one in the film. As such it presented greater challenges than what Arlen would later call the "lemon-drop" numbers written for the magical land of Oz. The genesis of "Over the

Rainbow" must be understood in light of the evolving conception at MGM of Dorothy's conflicted feelings about Kansas: Is it "home sweet home" or a place from which she must escape—or something of both?

KANSAS: "HOME SWEET HOME"?

The Kansas described at the beginning of L. Frank Baum's novel *The Wonderful Wizard of Oz* (1900), the original source for the film, is a grim place. The adjective "gray" appears ten times in the brief opening chapter and four times in the second paragraph alone:

> When Dorothy stood in the doorway and looked around, she could see nothing but the great gray prairie on every side. Not a tree nor a house broke the broad sweep of flat country that reached to the edge of the sky in all directions. The sun had baked the plowed land into a gray mass, with little cracks running through it. Even the grass was not green, for the sun had burned the tops of the long blades until they were the same gray color to be seen everywhere. Once the house had been painted, but the sun blistered the paint and the rains washed it away, and now the house was as dull and gray as everything else.[2]

Auntie Em personifies this dreary landscape. Her eyes, cheeks, and lips are also "gray"; she is "thin and gaunt and never smiled, now" (12). Auntie Em becomes a still more forbidding figure in the early screenplay drafts for *The Wizard of Oz*. There, she acts harshly and even cruelly toward Dorothy, who says of her, "She never really wanted me here."[3] Although her character softens in subsequent versions of the script, Auntie Em remains a dour presence.

In Baum's book the grayness of Kansas and Auntie Em may reflect the economic depression that affected the United States in the mid-1890s as a result of the financial crash in 1893. Some historians have interpreted *The Wonderful Wizard of Oz* as an allegory of contemporary politics that promotes the agrarian, anticapitalist values of the Populist movement and especially of the candidate William Jennings Bryan in the presidential election of 1896. (In fact, evidence suggests that Baum leaned politically the other way, as a supporter of the Republican William McKinley.)[4]

The Kansas of MGM's *The Wizard of Oz* reflects the deeper and longer depression America suffered in the 1930s, and it hints at the grim reality of the Dust Bowl, which devastated farms in portions of the state. The Kansas scenes were filmed in sepia tones, which arguably call greater attention to the bleakness of the landscape than would familiar black-and-white.

Harburg, whose left-leaning political beliefs would get him blacklisted in the 1950s, was ideally equipped to capture this bleak world of Kansas. In 1932 he had written the lyrics for the most iconic song of the Great Depression, "Brother, Can You Spare a Dime?" (music by Jay Gorney). In 1981 he claimed that in the film the Emerald City represented the New Deal, which would help, or at least promised to help, people escape the Depression.[5] Some commentators have also suggested that Frank Morgan's Wizard, whose screenplay lines were partly written by Harburg, is a gentle parody of Franklin Delano Roosevelt, who sought to encourage and empower the public, as the Wizard does Dorothy and her companions. Roosevelt often began his speeches with the same phrase—"My friends"—that the Wizard uses when addressing the citizens of the Emerald City in the last scene in Oz.[6]

For all its dreariness, Kansas is clearly home for Dorothy. At one point in Baum's original book, she has a conversation with the Scarecrow:

> "Tell me something about yourself and the country you came from," said the Scarecrow, when she had finished her dinner. So she told him all about Kansas, and how gray everything was there, and how the cyclone had carried her to this queer Land of Oz.
>
> The Scarecrow listened carefully, and said, "I cannot understand why you should wish to leave this beautiful country and go back to the dry, gray place you call Kansas."
>
> "That is because you have no brains," answered the girl. "No matter how dreary and gray our homes are, we people of flesh and blood would rather live there than in any other country, be it ever so beautiful. There is no place like home." (44)

Although everything in Kansas is "gray" even by her own admission, Dorothy staunchly defends her home. The theme of no place like home would feature strongly—and literally—in the development of the film and "Over the Rainbow."

From the earliest versions of the *Wizard of Oz* screenplay, crafted mainly by Noel Langley, Dorothy was to have a Kansas song. In March or April 1938, well before Arlen and Harburg were signed to the film, Roger Edens, a composer in Freed's unit at MGM and also a coach and mentor for Garland, had started to write a song entitled "Home Sweet Home in Kansas." The refrain (for which only lyrics survive) went:

Mid pleasures and palaces
In London, Paris, and Rome,

There is no place quite like Kansas
And my little Kansas home-sweet-home.[7]

Edens makes a direct allusion to "Home! Sweet Home!," a song composed in 1823 by Henry Bishop to a text by John Howard Payne. (Listen to example 1.1 ▶.) The first two lines run:

Mid pleasures and palaces though we may roam,
Be it ever so humble, there's no place like home.

"Home! Sweet Home!" has been called the most popular song of the nineteenth century, when it sold hundreds of thousands of sheet-music copies and was performed by many renowned singers.[8] Dozens of later songs made reference to "Home! Sweet Home!," capitalizing on its strong cultural appeal.[9] Thus it is not surprising that Edens would evoke it in his Kansas number for Dorothy.

The number that would eventually occupy the Kansas slot in *The Wizard of Oz* makes no reference to the idea of "home sweet home," in either music or lyrics. Arlen and Harburg's "Over the Rainbow" is about escape, about leaving home, and as such is surely different from what Edens and his colleagues originally envisioned. Yet the film's background score, composed by Herbert Stothart, included numerous allusions to the Bishop melody, especially in the final scene in Oz, when Glinda commands Dorothy to tap together her ruby slippers and repeat the phrase "There's no place like home."

A placeholder for Edens's Kansas song was slotted into a screenplay draft for *The Wizard of Oz* prepared by Langley on May 4, 1938. Langley specifies a "truck shot," where a camera follows Dorothy horizontally left or right as she is "walking along a row of hen roosts with a basket of eggs swinging in her hand, and Toto following behind, singing the Kansas song."[10]

For the scene in which Dorothy arrives in Oz, Edens also drafted a set of musical numbers, upon which Arlen and Harburg would later model their own extended Munchkinland sequence. Research by Arlen scholar Laura Lynn Broadhurst shows that in Edens's version of this sequence, as reflected in Langley's screenplay of May 4, Dorothy was to reprise her Kansas song when describing her home to Glinda and the Munchkins.[11] Among Edens's papers is a musical sketch for this number, entitled "My Castle in Kansas." Its fragmentary lyrics differ from those for "Home Sweet Home in Kansas," but the tune gives a good idea of the jaunty style that Edens envisioned (example 1.1).[12]

EXAMPLE 1.1 Roger Edens, sketch for Kansas number reprise in Munchkinland (Edens Collection, University of Southern California, Cinematic Arts Library)

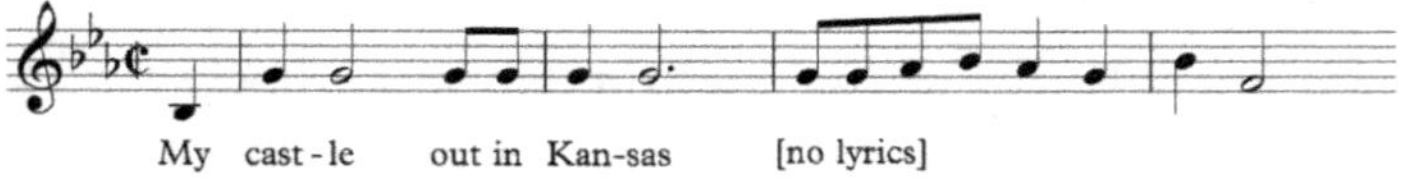

In early June Freed and LeRoy, dissatisfied with the screenplay of *The Wizard of Oz*, removed Langley and brought two new writers onto the project, Florence Ryerson and Edgar Allan Woolf. An experienced team who had already produced scripts for MGM, they would eventually share credit with Langley for the film. After reading Langley's script, Ryerson and Woolf objected to "a total lack of any real emotion," especially in the Oz scenes, which were filled with elaborate effects and actions peripheral to the central plot line of Dorothy's quest to return home. Ryerson and Woolf advised:

> All the emotions should be built up and intensified. This is especially true of Dorothy. We feel her desperate desire to get home should be dramatized more fully so that the various things which happen to prevent her from attaining her end are pointed up as terrifically important to the story.[13]

Ryerson and Woolf made changes to the opening scenes, seeking among other things to refine the nature and dramatic function of Dorothy's Kansas song. In a screenplay draft of June 9, 1938, Dorothy tells the farmhands Hunk and Hickory (played in the film by Ray Bolger and Jack Haley, who would double, respectively, as the Scarecrow and Tin Man) that she considers running away from the farm. The screenplay reads:

> HUNK: Go away <u>where</u>?
>
> DOROTHY: I don't know where . . . but I'm sure there's <u>some</u> place. . . there <u>must</u> be.
>
> NOTE: Here is where we plan to cue into our number. As discussed yesterday, this will be a song in which Dorothy tells how she is sure there is a land somewhere . . . a land where everything is lovely, where everyone is happy . . . the most beautiful place in the world. Or, perhaps it isn't in the world. Perhaps it's in a star. . . . In other words, when she sings this song <u>now</u>, she believes that this land is far away. But when

> she reprises on it in the Oz Sequences, she has learned that the land she is singing about is Kansas . . . the farm . . . home. Which lends it pathos.

The folksy, homespun number imagined by Ryerson and Woolf is far from what "Over the Rainbow" would become, as is made clear by the continuation of the note:

> The music is started by Hunk, who produces another harmonica (the one Aunt Em took away from him yesterday), and by Hickory, who uses his hammer, a piece of sandpaper, etc., on his metal contraption to get a novel musical effect. This, of course, leads into an orchestral accompaniment.[14]

Despite Ryerson and Woolf's attempt here to clarify the rationale for the Kansas number, the argument of which was elaborated in several subsequent screenplay drafts during June 1938, their note presents a garbled picture of Dorothy's emotions: she wants to get away, but it turns out the land she dreams of is really "home" after all.

Ryerson and Woolf continued to develop the "home sweet home" idea throughout July 1938, including in the last scene in Oz, where Dorothy clicks her ruby slippers together three times and repeats "There's no place like home." (The use of that specific phrase was apparently Freed's idea.) After she wakes up in Kansas, Dorothy says, in the final lines of one draft, "Isn't it funny—this is the place I was looking for all the time! And I never knew it! This is the most beautiful place in the whole wide world!"[15]

When Harburg came up with his own concept for the Kansas song, he had little use for these portrayals of Dorothy's attitude toward her home. His feelings did not change when he became actively involved in drafting or revising dialogue for the screenplay in mid-July. As Harburg would later tell the *Wizard of Oz* historian Aljean Harmetz, "The picture didn't need that 'Home, Sweet Home,' 'God Bless Our Home' tripe."[16] Harburg preferred Langley's scripts to those of Ryerson and Woolf, and it was he who pressured Freed into rehiring Langley at the end of July. Langley proceeded to rewrite much of Ryerson and Woolf's screenplay.

Because LeRoy and Freed liked the "home sweet home" concept, it continued to loom large in *The Wizard of Oz*, as it would, mutatis mutandis, in other Hollywood films of the era, including *Gone With the Wind*, released the same year (1939), and *It's a Wonderful Life* (1946).[17] Yet the presence of "Over the Rainbow" in *The Wizard of Oz* largely undermines such sentiments. There *is* no place like home, but if one's physical home is an unhappy place, one must seek a new home in the land beyond the rainbow.

ARLEN AND HARBURG SET TO WORK

In Hollywood of the 1930s composers and lyricists were contract workers who had little if any input into the development of a screenplay. Songs were rarely integrated into the narrative of film. Freed wanted a different kind of score for *The Wizard of Oz*, in which each song would grow directly out of the plot and reflect the situations and emotions of the characters. Harburg's close involvement with the screenplay, as well as his authorship of the lyrics, helped

The Wizard of Oz achieve this kind of integration of music and narrative.

As they began to work on the songs for *The Wizard of Oz* in May 1938, Arlen and Harburg followed a routine typical for their collaborations. Harburg would come up with a poetic idea, an image, or a title for a song, based on an important element of the plot. He would present it to Arlen, who would then compose most or all of the music, to which Harburg would then fit lyrics.

The first song Arlen and Harburg completed for *The Wizard of Oz*, "The Jitterbug," was probably intended to realize a concept from the earliest stages in the evolution of the film, of Dorothy as "an orphan in Kansas who sings jazz."[18] Evoking a popular style of swing dance, "The Jitterbug" was planned for a scene in the haunted forest when the Witch sends biting insects that make Dorothy and her companions jump and "jitter." The scene was shot but ultimately cut from *The Wizard of Oz* after previews, when the film was deemed too long.

Although "The Jitterbug" was dropped, most of the remaining songs in *The Wizard of Oz* are dance-related, including the march-like "Ding-Dong! The Witch Is Dead" and "We're Off to See the Wizard," the waltz "Come Out, Come Out, Wherever You Are," and the soft-shoe "If I Only Had a Brain," which was a repurposed number cut from Arlen and Harburg's Broadway show *Hooray for What?* "Over the Rainbow" is the outlier, a ballad of longing that proved more challenging for Arlen and Harburg to write.

By the end of April 1938 Freed made clear that however much he liked the "home sweet home" idea, he did not favor Edens's approach to Dorothy's Kansas number. Freed wanted a ballad modeled on the song "Someday My Prince Will Come" from the 1937 Disney animated feature *Snow White and the Seven Dwarfs*, which MGM sought to surpass with *The Wizard of Oz*. (View example 1.2 ▶.) In a memo, Freed wrote: "The whole love story in *Snow White* is motivated by the song 'Some Day My Prince Will Come' as Snow White is looking into the well."[19] Freed was conflating two songs in this comment. Snow White sings "I'm Wishing" into a well at the very opening of the film, while "Someday My Prince Will Come" appears later, sung to the dwarves by the fireplace.

In fact, both "I'm Wishing" and "Someday My Prince Will Come" are classic "I want" songs. This is a type of number, usually but not always found near the beginning of a show or film, which expresses the desires that will motivate the protagonist's actions. Eliza Doolittle's "Wouldn't It Be Loverly" from *My Fair Lady* (1956) is one prominent example, Elphaba's "The Wizard and I" from *Wicked* (2003) a later one. Because the universality of its message has allowed it to be detached from the original dramatic context, "Over the Rainbow" remains one of the best-known and beloved "I want" songs.

Whether or not they saw the Freed memo, Arlen and Harburg were aware of his evolving concept for the Kansas number. Over the years, both would frequently be asked about the origins of "Over the Rainbow," their most famous song. Harburg tended to embellish and modify his version; Arlen was more consistent, but also more laconic. On some points they contradict each other. Yet from their accounts and other sources a plausible outline of the genesis of the song can be fleshed out.

Harburg claimed that the grayness of Baum's Kansas inspired the image of a rainbow for Dorothy's song. As he told an interviewer in 1980:

> This particular ballad was a ballad for a little girl who . . . was in trouble, and like all little girls wanted to get away from where she was at. And where was she at? Kansas. A dry, arid colorless place. She had never seen anything colorful in her life except the rainbow. Well, where would a little girl like that, not knowing the world, want to go? Over that rainbow. On the other side of the rainbow. . . . And I told Harold about it, and he went to work on a tune.[20]

Harburg presented Arlen with a tentative title, "Over the Rainbow Is Where I Want to Be."

For his part, Arlen recalled, "I felt we needed something with sweep, a melody with a long broad line."[21] He was a musical perfectionist who often struggled to find just the right melody, harmony, and structure for a song. He would carry around in his pocket blank pieces of music paper. When inspiration struck, he would write down short melodic ideas he called "jots." Arlen was especially anxious to find the right tune and mood for Dorothy's ballad, as he explained in his most extended recollection of the song's musical inception:

> We had finished most of the songs, all of the songs but the one for Judy in Kansas—the one for [the] Dorothy character in Kansas, and I knew what I wanted. Arthur Freed, the associate producer, couldn't understand what I was worried about. Most people don't understand what you're worried about because they think you do this and out it comes. But when you have to labor, most writers don't like that. It's nice to be gentle

about gettin' at the piano and, you know, foolin' around a little while and coming up with an idea. But when it doesn't come, it becomes one of those things that bug ya. And most of us don't like to be bugged, not too long.

And I said to Mrs. Arlen, I said, "Let's go to Grauman's Chinese [Theatre]." I said, "You drive the car. I don't feel too well right now." I wasn't thinking of work. I wasn't conscious of thinking of work. I just wanted to relax. And as we drove by Schwab's Drug Store on Sunset [Boulevard], I said, "Pull over, please." And she knew what I meant, and we stopped and I really don't know why, bless the muses, and I took out my little piece of manuscript and put down what you know now as "Over the Rainbow." Of course, it needed Mr. Harburg's lyric.[22]

Arlen told his biographer Edward Jablonski of the relief that came over him: "It was as if the Lord said, 'Well, here it is, now stop worrying about it.' "[23] Arlen's inspiration for the opening of "Over the Rainbow" may have involved a subconscious lyrical transformation of the initial gesture of "The Jitterbug," an upward octave leap followed by a downward half step (see brackets in example 1.2). (Almost a decade after *The Wizard of Oz*, Richard Rodgers would use the same melodic figure for "Bali Hai" in *South Pacific*.)

EXAMPLE 1.2 Opening melodic gestures of "Over the Rainbow" and "The Jitterbug"

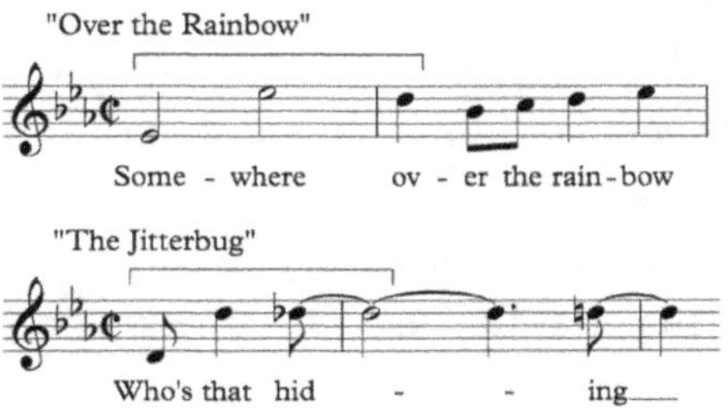

After his moment of inspiration at Schwab's Drugstore, Arlen returned to his house in the Hollywood Hills and wrote a song in the standard thirty-two-bar AABA form of popular music (more on this in chapter 3). The next day he called Harburg over to listen. When Arlen played the A segment on the piano with symphonic sweep and bravura, Harburg balked, suggesting that it seemed more appropriate for an opera singer (he mentioned the singer and film star Nelson Eddy) than for a girl from Kansas.

After Harburg registered his initial disappointment with the A section of "Over the Rainbow," the composer and the lyricist called a friend, Ira Gershwin, to come over and listen to the tune. When Ira suggested that Arlen play the song with greater moderation and rhythmic clarity, Harburg was won over. In addition to helping mediate between Arlen and Harburg, Gershwin appears to have contributed the words for the coda of "Over the Rainbow." He told Michael Feinstein that the composer and lyricist were struggling to come up with a final line, and Ira suggested the line we know today, beginning "If happy little bluebirds fly . . ." Feinstein asked Ira why he had "chimed in." Ira replied, "They'd been working at the piano for a long, long, time, and I wanted to make it a short evening."[24]

Arlen composed the B, or bridge, section in a simpler style, as a kind of foil to the sophistication of the main melody. In later years Harburg claimed that the bridge melody, oscillating between two notes, was inspired by the tune Arlen would whistle to call his dog. But Arlen disputed this memory, saying that he based the bridge on the idea of a child's piano exercise.[25]

HARBURG'S LYRICS

When writing the lyrics for "Over the Rainbow" Harburg likely worked from an undated lead sheet in Arlen's hand, on which the melodic line of the song as we know it is written out or accounted for in the key of E flat (figure 1.2).[26]

FIGURE 1.2 Harold Arlen, autograph lead sheet for "Over the Rainbow" (Harburg Collection, Irving Gilmore Music Library, Yale University)

At this point, the song had no "verse," or introductory section; this was added later and would not be sung in the film, although it would appear in the published sheet music.

Harburg recalled that his greatest challenge came with Arlen's upward octave leap at the beginning of the melody:

> He gave me a tune with those first two notes. I tried "*I'll go over the rainbow*," "*Some day over the rainbow*," or "*the other side of the rainbow*." I had difficulty coming to the idea of "*Somewhere*." For a while I just thought I would leave those first two notes out. It was a long time before I came to "*Somewhere over the rainbow*."[27]

In another interview Harburg described how and why he got the idea of using long vowels to convey the sense of yearning and distance implied by Arlen's opening octave leap:

> I was given a tune [in] which, for the first part, I couldn't use consonants. I couldn't write, "Say Bud." It wouldn't sing. You have to use open vowels. "Somewhere o-ver the rainbow. . . ." The "o" comes right in—that is an important part of the writing. So, on top of the playfulness of the words, on top of the meaning and the poetry, the sound has an importance.
>
> Somewhere ōver the rāinbōw
> Wāy up hīgh
> or: Skīes are blūe[28]

Two pages of lyric drafts for the bridge section of "Over the Rainbow" reveal something of Harburg's working method (figure 1.3).[29] Harburg had the challenge of capturing the simpler mood of the child's piano exercise suggested by Arlen's music. He also had to fit lyrics to Arlen's

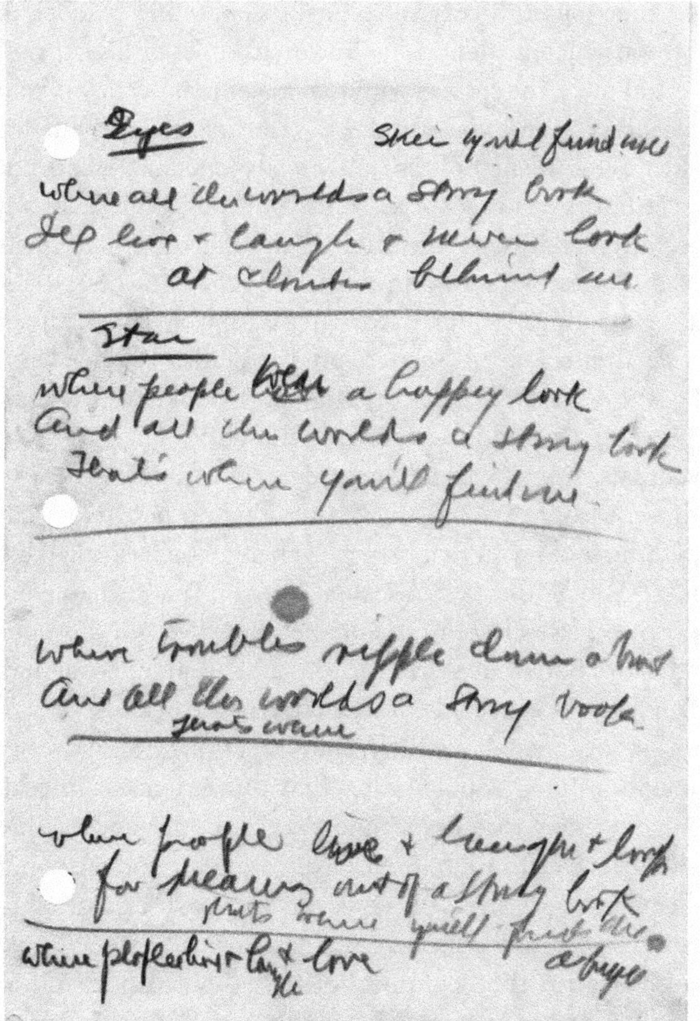

FIGURE 1.3 Harburg, drafts for bridge lyrics for "Over the Rainbow" (Harburg Collection, Irving Gilmore Music Library, Yale University)

two four-measure musical phrases that, while parallel, are not constructed identically. The first ends with two notes ("-hind me"), the second with four notes that occupy two full measures ("where you'll find me"). Harburg needed nineteen syllables for the first phrase and twenty-one for the second.

Harburg's headings "Eyes" and "Star" suggest that, as with the initial "rainbow" concept, he thought first in terms of basic images or themes to be developed. The verses below those headings, which have twenty-one syllables, appear to be drafts for the second phrase of the bridge. Under "Eyes": "Where all the world's a story book, / I'll live and laugh and never look / At clouds behind me." Harburg would eventually use "clouds behind me" for the first four-measure phrase. Under "Star" are three lines that do not in fact have anything to do with that image: "Where people wear a happy look / And all the world's a story book, / That's where you'll find me." Here Harburg maintained but reversed the "look" and "story book" ideas from "Eyes," and he added what in the completed song became the final line of the bridge.

The jottings below the "Star" section (in figure 1.3) introduce the "trouble" idea that also made it into the song: "Where troubles ripple down about" and "Where troubles never think to look." Even allowing for the benefit of hindsight, admirers of "Over the Rainbow" can admit the rightness of Harburg's decision to drop the "story book / look" idea for the beginning of the second bridge phrase and to refine the "trouble" concept into "Where troubles melt like lemon drops" and its paired rhyme "Away above the chimney tops."

No precise date can be established for the completion of "Over the Rainbow," but it must have been before June 24, 1938, which Broadhurst has confirmed as the date when it was first slotted into the screenplay drafts of *The Wizard of Oz* as Dorothy's Kansas number, replacing the earlier "no place like home" placeholder. The first MGM in-house piano-vocal score of "Over the Rainbow" is dated June 29. The score is identified as being "transcribed by Sam Messenheimer," an MGM staff musician who, as we also know from Broadhurst's research, served as an assistant charged with copying down the songs from Arlen's playing.[30] This score, which corresponds closely to the version of the song that Garland sings in the film, was registered for copyright with the Library of Congress on July 18. (A later MGM piano-vocal score of "Over the Rainbow," dated August 12, 1938, has the verse in place of the spoken lead-in. Arlen and Harburg created it for the eventual publication of the sheet music.) Yet as we will see in the next chapter, "Over the Rainbow" had not yet attained the definitive shape it would assume in *The Wizard of Oz.*

CHAPTER 2
BRINGING THE RAINBOW TO LIFE

THE MAKING OF *The Wizard of Oz* encountered many roadblocks and extended almost a year beyond the summer of 1938. The film had four successive directors, Richard Thorpe, George Cukor, Victor Fleming, and King Vidor. There were frequent cast changes, the most famous involving Jack Haley assuming the role of the Tin Man when the silver makeup and body paint sickened Buddy Ebsen. Serious injuries plagued the production. Margaret Hamilton had to miss over a month on the set after suffering first- and second-degree burns when filming the exit of the Wicked Witch of the West from the Munchkin village.

As for "Over the Rainbow," although Arlen and Harburg completed the definitive score of the song by the end of June

1938, part of its lyrics remained in flux, as did the directors' and screenwriters' ideas for reprising the song after the Kansas scene. The MGM creative team also explored potential realizations in Technicolor of the song's central image of the rainbow.

THE ALTERNATE BRIDGE LYRICS

One of the most striking—and puzzling—aspects of the development of "Over the Rainbow" in *The Wizard of Oz* is that two different versions of the lyrics for the B section, or bridge, persisted in parallel for many months. The lyrics as we know them today appear in the manuscript score of June 29, 1938 (mentioned in chapter 1), and in the piano-vocal score published by Leo Feist, Inc., in the summer of 1939. Garland used them when she pre-recorded "Over the Rainbow" for the film's soundtrack on October 7, 1938:

> Someday I'll wish upon a star
> And wake up where the clouds are far behind me.
> Where troubles melt like lemon drops,
> Away above the chimney tops,
> That's where you'll find me.

But in the June 24 screenplay draft—the first in which the song is slotted in—the bridge reads:

> Someday I'll wake and rub my eyes
> And in that land beyond the skies you'll find me.

I'll be a laughin' daffodil
And leave the silly cares that fill my mind behind me.[1]

The June 24 screenplay also lacks any indication of the song's coda ("If happy little bluebirds fly . . .").

One might assume that the "rub my eyes" lyrics represent an early version of the bridge that Harburg gave the screenwriters sometime in mid-June but that he revised by the time of the June 29 piano-vocal score. Yet this alternate version of the bridge lyrics continues to appear (and the coda is absent) in all screenplay versions of the Kansas scene right through the final shooting script for *The Wizard of Oz* of October 10, 1938.[2] They are still present as of February 1, 1939.[3] Only with the continuity script of March 15, 1939, do the proper lyrics and the coda of "Over the Rainbow" seem at last to be in place.[4]

The final bridge lyrics seem much preferable to these alternate ones. Harburg had explored both the "eyes" and "star" images in the sketches discussed in chapter 1. In the version of June 24 we have the former ("rub my eyes"), and in the final version the latter ("Someday I'll wish upon a star"). In the final version Harburg also replaces "skies" with "clouds" and he reverses the "find me / behind me" rhyme of lines 2 and 4 to make what is arguably a more effective succession. Perhaps most important (and beneficially), the final version abandons the "laughin' daffodil" and "silly cares" images that seem alien to the serious spirit of the rest of the words and of Arlen's actual music.

In screenplay drafts the alternate bridge lyrics persisted not only for Dorothy's farmyard performance of "Over the

Rainbow" but also for one of the planned reprises of the song, to which we now turn.

THE "RAINBOW" REPRISES

On June 29, 1938, the producer LeRoy's assistant William Cannon prepared a memo that showed the intended placement of all the songs that had been written so far for *The Wizard of Oz.* After its initial appearance in the Kansas scene, "Over the Rainbow" was to be reprised three more times: in Munchkinland, later in the film in the Witch's Castle, and at the very end during a fade-out from the Kansas farm to the credits.[5]

We can see from the drafts by Ryerson and Woolf that the Munchkinland reprise planned by Edens for his Kansas song "Home Sweet Home in Kansas," present in the earlier screenplay draft by Langley from May 4, has been reduced to a brief, partial reappearance of "Over the Rainbow." Dorothy introduces it with her now immortal line as she steps into Oz for the first time and sees an actual rainbow:

> DOROTHY (*to Toto*): Toto, I've got a feeling we're not in Kansas any more. (*Her eyes widen, as she sees fresh beauty on every side.*) Isn't it wonderful? (*Looks up and discovers a beautiful rainbow.*) Look! We must be over the rainbow! (*She begins singing dreamily to the music.*)
>
> There's a land that I heard of
> Once in a lullaby.[6]

In the filmed version of this scene no rainbow is visible in Oz, and "Over the Rainbow" is reduced to a few phrases in the orchestral underscoring.

On October 17, 1938, ten days after she had pre-recorded "Over the Rainbow" in a sound studio with Herbert Stothart and the MGM orchestra, Garland went onto the set of *The Wizard of Oz* to film and record a partial reprise that featured the alternate bridge lyrics. The reprise occurs in the Witch's Castle, after the witch turns over the hourglass and leaves the captive Dorothy alone. Because the screenplay directs Dorothy to break down sobbing, Garland could not easily pre-record or lip-sync the reprise. It was thus captured directly on the *Oz* set, with Roger Edens accompanying Garland on an off-screen piano.[7] Stothart would record the orchestral underscoring for this reprise many months later, on May 6, 1939, which reveals that, though eventually cut, the alternate version was still in the film at an advanced stage of production.[8]

In the on-set recording, Edens plays the entire A section of "Over the Rainbow" as an instrumental solo, after which Garland enters with a tearful rendition of the first two lines of the alternate bridge: "Someday I'll wake and rub my eyes, / And in that land beyond the skies you'll find me." (Listen to example 2.1 ▶.) She breaks down while the accompaniment continues for the second part of the bridge. Then through her sobs (with no accompaniment by Edens, but later with underscoring by Stothart), Garland attempts to reprise the last A section of the song. But she falters on "Why then, oh why," leaving the phrase unfinished. Here the screenwriters understood that the lines with "laughin' daffodil" and "silly cares" would be inappropriate in a such a moment of despair and therefore had Garland weep her way wordlessly through that segment.

This reprise of "Over the Rainbow" was to be only one element of a larger role for the song and its imagery in the Witch's Castle episodes of *The Wizard of Oz*. In early July 1938 the screenwriters Ryerson and Woolf drafted a scene, for which a full scenario survives, that involved an illusory rainbow bridge conjured by the Wicked Witch to tempt Dorothy to escape from the castle but then fall to her death.[9]

The immediate impetus for the witch's action would have been yet another planned reprise of "Over the Rainbow" shortly after the tearful one discussed above. The Scarecrow, the Tin Man, and the Cowardly Lion are climbing up the rocks toward the castle to rescue Dorothy when they hear her singing "Over the Rainbow." We cut to the inside of a tower room, where the witch also hears Dorothy singing, through a closed window:

> WITCH: Mocking me by singing, eh?
>
> *She pushes the window open furiously, just in time to get the end of the* SONG: Birds fly over the rainbow—why then, oh why can't I? *A cruel smile lights her face.*
>
> WITCH (*cont'd*): So she wants to go over the rainbow, does she?

The witch opens a parchment scroll, labeled, in "ancient script": "Spells for making Rain . . . Raindrops . . . Rainbows." To cast the spell, she begins to read rhymed couplets. At this point the screenplay notes, "Mr. Harburg is working out these rhymes for us." Although no such lyrics survive, it is no surprise that Ryerson and Woolf turned to Harburg, whose mastery of the couplet style is evident from the Munchkinland sequence ("As Coroner I must aver, / I thoroughly examined her, / And she's not only merely dead, / She's really most sincerely dead").

While the witch is casting the spell, the Scarecrow, Tin Man, and Cowardly Lion enter the castle disguised as Winkie guards. They overhear "Over the Rainbow" being hummed by someone they assume to be Dorothy, then tip-toe into the room from which the sound is coming, only to discover it is the witch humming as she brews her spell. The Winkies seize the three visitors, and the witch makes them watch as she waves her broomstick to create the illusory bridge stretching between her room and the tower where Dorothy is being held captive. The scene, perhaps inspired in part by the rainbow bridge at the end of Wagner's *Das Rheingold*, would have been a Technicolor wonder, as described by Ryerson and Woolf:

> A rainbow has formed a bridge between the two towers. This is very long and passes across the whole courtyard, which is a great distance below. It is a beautiful sight, but like all rainbows, it grows thinner and thinner as it curves upward. The general effect is like one of those lovely curved bridges in Venice.

The witch decides to test out the bridge by sending one of her Winkie guards across it, purportedly to fetch Dorothy. The Winkie plunges to his death through the center of the rainbow, and the witch cruelly exults at the success of her spell. She then forces the Scarecrow and the Tin Man to call out to Dorothy. As Dorothy hears their voices, Ryerson and Woolf engage in a bit of hypothetical musical composition: "The rainbow music is playing softly on the SOUNDTRACK with, possibly, the witch's theme in counter melody to give it menace."

Dorothy runs up to the top of the tower to find the source of the sound, and then, "with a glad cry, she starts up the side of the rainbow bridge." She suddenly realizes the danger she is in, but her ruby slippers "seem to come to life with an iridescent glow. They run across the perilous center of the bridge as though carrying her with them." She runs down the descending part of the bridge and into the arms of her friends. The witch's plot has been foiled.

When Langley was brought back onto *The Wizard of Oz* as a screenwriter at the end of July 1938, he dumped Ryerson and Woolf's rainbow bridge scene, which would have been too costly and technically challenging even for this lavish production. Dorothy's tearful reprise of "Over the Rainbow" in the Witch's Castle would eventually end up on the cutting room floor. Even the partial return in Munchkinland was never realized in any form.

In *The Wizard of Oz*, only one substantial reprise of "Over the Rainbow," for orchestra alone, remains from those outlined in the Cannon memo of June 29. The song is heard complete (but without coda) in the underscoring of the final scene of the film, when Dorothy wakes up in Kansas and tries to explain to her concerned but skeptical listeners where she has been.

Thus "Over the Rainbow" appears only in the Kansas scenes that bookend the film. This placement surely resulted less from some larger, consistent musico-dramatic vision on the part of the creative team than from a series of practical editing decisions made over many months. Yet, since "Over the Rainbow" expresses longing to escape Kansas, not celebrate its virtues, the ballad makes most sense when sung or heard in Kansas. That is where the Kansas song belongs and where, ultimately, it remained.

FILMING "OVER THE RAINBOW"

Dorothy's farmyard scene has become almost as iconic as the song itself. She performs "Over the Rainbow" as a private, almost prayerful number that is shared with no one but Toto—and us, her viewers. This scene is very different from that envisioned by Ryerson and Woolf, who had replaced Langley's Dorothy-among-the-hen-roosts scenario with one in which she tells the farmhands Hickory and Hunk of her idea to run away from home. She sings her Kansas song to them in response to their questions and reactions ("Where would you run to?" and "There ain't no such place"). In some Ryerson/Woolf drafts that were written before "Over the Rainbow" was slotted in, as noted above, the farmhands actually participate in the song.

Only in a very late screenplay revision of February 1, 1939, does the definitive dramatic scenario for "Over the Rainbow" seem to emerge.[10] Here, after hearing the story of Dorothy falling into the pigpen, Auntie Em impatiently sends Hickory and Hunk back to work (but also gives them some fresh crullers she's baked). Zeke (Bert Lahr), the third farmhand, who was not present in earlier drafts, also departs, as does Auntie Em herself, leaving Dorothy alone with Toto.

"Over the Rainbow" became a soliloquy, the only number in *The Wizard of Oz* that Dorothy is not singing to anyone within the plot. "Over the Rainbow" thus departs from its putative model, "Someday My Prince Will Come," which Snow White sings to the dwarfs gathered around the fireplace. During the song they are often on camera, reacting and even interjecting comments ("Mush," says Grumpy, sitting in a corner with his back turned to the group). Nor is another possible model from the Disney film, Snow White's opening song, "I'm Wishing," a real soliloquy, since the white doves who listen to her react anthropomorphically, nodding their heads when she asks them, "Want to know a secret?"

The sepia-tinted farmyard scene of *The Wizard of Oz*, among the last to be filmed, was directed by King Vidor, who took over in February 1939, when MGM pulled Fleming to work on *Gone with the Wind*. Vidor was involved with *The Wizard of Oz* for only ten days and was responsible mainly for the opening Kansas scenes. He was rightly proud of his achievement in the two-and-a-half-minute sequence of "Over the Rainbow." (View example 2.2 ▶.) As he later told Harmetz, "I staged 'Over the Rainbow' with Judy walking. Previous to this, when people sang, they stood still. I used 'Over the Rainbow' to get some rhythmical flow of movement into a ballad."[11] Elsewhere, Vidor recalled his own conscious attempt to capture the style of a silent movie in keeping "the movement of Judy Garland flowing freely."[12] Vidor's fluid direction reinforces the strong integration of songs into the narrative flow, one of the film's most distinctive innovations.

The spoken lead-in to "Over the Rainbow" is underscored by Stothart's beautiful fifteen-measure introduction, the last musical element of the song to be recorded (April 13, 1939). When Dorothy says, "It's not a place you can get to by a boat or a train"—at exactly the moment she imagines the trouble-free zone Auntie Em told her to find—she begins to walk forward, and the camera pulls back with her. When she realizes the place is "far, far away," Dorothy turns her gaze upward, where it will remain focused for much of the song.

Vidor is extraordinarily sensitive to the poetic-musical structure of "Over the Rainbow" (to be examined more closely in the next chapter). Dorothy's movements and the angle of her gaze are closely coordinated with the segments of the song's thirty-two bar form, AABA (plus coda). Vidor keeps Dorothy walking throughout the spoken introduction and into the first A. As she sings, Dorothy turns to her right (viewer's left) around a haystack and then leans back against it (at the phrase "way up high"). She pauses there for the rest of the A section. This pattern of motion-then-pause is repeated for the next two segments of the song (AB). The form is also articulated by Dorothy's looking down at or near the beginning of a segment, focusing at first on her immediate surroundings, before turning her eyes upward again to the skies (on "skies are blue," in the second A).

Vidor articulates the beginning of the B section ("Someday I'll wish upon a star") by cutting away from Dorothy for the first time, to Toto. Dorothy is once again in motion, at first swinging gently back and forth with both arms on the large wheel of the horse-drawn hay rake, then walking around it. In keeping with the B section as the contrasting part of the song form, Dorothy's eyes remain focused mostly downward, often on Toto. After the fourth measure ("behind me"), as in the A segments, she stops; she pets Toto, who is perched on the seat of the rake, turns around, and sits down on the long wooden arm that would be used to connect the rake to the horses.

For the final A, as if to mark that the song is coming to a close, Vidor breaks the previous pattern: Dorothy remains seated throughout, her eyes turned upward (figure 2.1). At the end of the section she directs to Toto the only actual question of the song ("Why then, oh why can't I?") and shakes his proffered paw. Vidor marks the coda ("If happy little bluebirds fly"), as he did the start of B, by turning the camera away from Dorothy, upward to the light streaming through a break in the clouds. For the first time the viewer is made to look up with Dorothy (instead of watching her

FIGURE 2.1 Dorothy begins the reprise (the final A) of "Over the Rainbow" in *The Wizard of Oz*

look up) and begins to understand that something special may indeed lie behind the clouds. "Over the Rainbow" is as much a filmic triumph for Vidor as it is a musical and poetic one for Arlen and Harburg.

"THE SONG STAYS—OR I GO!"

It is one of the most frequently told yet hard-to-believe stories about the making of *The Wizard of Oz*: "Over the Rainbow" was cut during previews of the film. By June 1939, with filming and editing complete, *The Wizard of Oz* ran almost two hours, a good thirty minutes longer than the average Hollywood film at the time. The producer LeRoy and director Fleming knew that some trimming was necessary, and they used several sneak previews around southern California as opportunities to explore cuts. The first sequence to go was "The Jitterbug," probably because the lively, elaborate dance number was deemed inappropriate at a tense moment in the film, when the Wicked Witch is pursuing Dorothy and her companions. Also dropped was an extended dance sequence for Ray Bolger as the Scarecrow, during the number "If I Only Had a Brain."

"Over the Rainbow" was cut in a preview in Pomona, California, on June 16. Freed and LeRoy both later recalled that several MGM executives wanted the song out because it slowed down the picture; they also wondered why Garland should have to sing a ballad in a farmyard. By most accounts it was Freed who rescued "Over the Rainbow." At a meeting called by the studio chief Louis B. Mayer to settle the issue of "Rainbow," Freed said,

"The song stays—or I go! It's as simple as that."[13] By early July, "Over the Rainbow" was back in the film.

Harburg's retelling of the events around the cutting of "Over the Rainbow" is characteristically vivid. After attending the preview from which the song was dropped,

> Harold [Arlen] and I just went crazy. . . . We knew that this was the ballad of the show, good God. This is the number we were depending on. And we decided to take action. We went to the front office, we went to the back office, we pleaded, we cried, we tore our hair, Harold ran to *shul*. There wasn't a god around who could help us until finally Arthur Freed . . . realized the value of the song, went to Louis B. Mayer, pleaded with him. . . . Well, L. B. Mayer was very nice with Arthur Freed and said, "Aw, well . . . let the boys have the damn song. Put it back in the picture. It can't hurt."[14]

Arlen's biographer Jablonski paints a picture of somewhat greater passivity—or frustrated resignation—on Arlen's part. Arlen reported to Jablonski that he came home from a "Rainbow"-less preview and told his wife, "No more previews. From now on I'm just going to write the best I can, turn 'em in and forget 'em."[15] This statement accords well with the image one gets of Arlen across his career from various accounts: a composer who worked hard and understood the value of his creations, but who also saw himself as part of larger enterprises, especially in Hollywood, over which he could not or would not seek to exert control.

JUST "A VERY PRETTY SONG"

To follow another important thread of the "Rainbow" story, we need to return to the fall of 1938. All the main songs for

The Wizard of Oz were pre-recorded for the soundtrack between September 30 and October 11, 1938. The MGM studio and its music publishing arm, Leo Feist, Inc., wanted to keep a tight lid on the music until near the premiere of the film, at which point it was common for Hollywood studios to release preliminary copies of sheet music to recording artists as part of a promotional effort, soon to be followed by official publication. MGM was counting on *The Wizard of Oz* to be a big hit and planned an elaborate publicity roll-out. Because of many delays in the production, that moment would only come in the late spring and summer of 1939.

Sometime in late fall 1938, music for two numbers from the film, "The Jitterbug" and "Over the Rainbow" (perhaps copies of the studio piano-vocal manuscripts), came into the hands of a prominent bandleader on the East Coast, Larry Clinton, who arranged and recorded them for RCA Victor in New York on December 7, 1938. For "Jitterbug" Clinton teamed up with the vocalist Ford Leary. For "Rainbow" he partnered with Bea Wain, one of his regular collaborators and a well-regarded jazz singer (figure 2.2). (Listen to example 2.3 ▶.)

When Clinton and Wain recorded "Over the Rainbow," they would have been familiar with neither the dramatic context of the song nor Garland's soundtrack recording, which was in the can but months away from being filmed and still further from release. Their "Over the Rainbow" was created in a world far from Kansas and Oz: a world of big bands, jazz singers, and up-tempo foxtrots. ("Foxtrot," as "Over the Rainbow" was labeled on the RCA Clinton disk, was at this time the generic designation for any song in duple meter. An internal *Wizard of Oz* memo from

FIGURE 2.2 Larry Clinton and Bea Wain in the late 1930s

MGM categorizes "Over the Rainbow" as both a "foxtrot" and a "ballad.")

Clinton's tempo for "Over the Rainbow" is ♩ = 110, typical for the big-band style and much faster than Garland's soundtrack speed of ♩ = 88. After a short introduction, Clinton's band plays the chorus once through (minus the coda), featuring a smooth muted trombone on the melody for the A sections. Then Wain enters, singing the chorus with little fluctuation in tempo and in a strongly syncopated style, just ahead of the beat. Clinton plays the chorus one more time through, now really swung, featuring first a full saxophone choir, then a brass one.

In a brief interview in January 2014, Bea Wain, then ninety-seven years old, could not recall too much about her studio date with Clinton over seventy-five years earlier. But she did say that in December 1938 she was unfamiliar with the making of *Wizard of Oz*. "Over the Rainbow," she noted, "was just like any other thing I recorded. I knew nothing about it except it was a very pretty song."[16]

It is not clear how Clinton obtained the music for "Over the Rainbow" and "The Jitterbug." As an RCA artist, he may have had access to songs as a result of an early deal between Leo Feist and RCA to record all of *The Wizard of Oz* songs for an album.[17] That arrangement would have recalled another made not long before between RCA and Disney Studios. In January 1938, RCA Victor had issued a three-disk collection of songs from Disney's *Snow White and the Seven Dwarfs*, timed to coincide with the nationwide release of the animated film. For *The Wizard of Oz*, however, the soundtrack was still in progress in the fall of 1938. Decca would eventually release an album of songs from the film, newly recorded, in March 1940. (The soundtrack of *The Wizard of Oz* would in fact not be issued on record until the 1950s.)

To judge from the reactions of MGM and Feist to the Clinton recordings, no deal with RCA was ever finalized. Studio executives became almost immediately aware of the Clinton sessions of December 8. On December 13, 1938, Harry Link, the general manager of Feist in Los Angeles, wrote to RCA Victor, explaining that since the film was not scheduled for release before March 1939 at the earliest, "this letter is being sent to you . . . requesting that you make no releases of any of the recordings of the songs from this production, until such time as we notify you that

Metro-Goldwyn-Mayer has advised us to release the songs for exploitation."[18]

This missive began a long series of letters and cables that stretched well into the spring of 1939. Despite urgent communications to RCA from MGM and Link, on February 27, 1939, the record company released nationwide almost ten thousand copies of a disk with "Over the Rainbow" on one side and "The Jitterbug" on the other. In early March, RCA finally heeded the pleas from Feist and attempted to stop sales of the disk. But RCA had little authority over its distributors, which were mostly independent companies that had by then shipped almost five thousand copies to private music stores, outlets for which RCA had no list or contact information.

On April 18, the head of the MGM music department, Nat Finston, was dismayed to see a copy of the "Rainbow"/ "Jitterbug" disk for sale at Bullock's Department Store in Los Angeles. He bought it and notified the film's producer LeRoy and the studio head Louis B. Mayer. A day later, on April 19, Clinton and his band played "Jitterbug" live in Nashville, Tennessee, on a broadcast that was relayed across the country over the NBC radio network, including to California, where LeRoy's secretary heard it and brought it to the attention of her boss. He told MGM to issue a strong cease-and-desist order to Clinton.

For all of MGM's concern, the Clinton-Wain recording of "Over the Rainbow" did not attract much attention at the time from the public, at least not in the jazz press, where one would expect it. In *Metronome* magazine in April 1939, the critic George Simon, writing under the alias Gordon Wright, noted briefly, "There's pretty muted trumpeting and lovely Bea Wain singing in *Larry Clinton's Over the Rainbow*—the band's Gilbert-and-Sullivan take-offs don't click."[19] With "Gilbert-and-Sullivan take-offs" Simon may be referring to the oscillating pattern of the song's bridge. In "Some day I'll wish upon a star" he may have heard an unfortunate echo of something like the patter song "I Am the Very Model of a Modern Major General" from *The Pirates of Penzance*. Of course, in April 1939 Simon was still unfamiliar with *The Wizard of Oz* and Garland's soundtrack recording of "Over the Rainbow." The difference between the gentle tinkling of a child's piano exercise (Arlen's model for the bridge) and the parody of a Gilbert and Sullivan patter song would not be apparent from a jazz rendition.

GOOD NEWS: "RAINBOW" GOES OUT OVER THE AIRWAVES

Although there was little to be done about the Clinton recordings or broadcasts, MGM moved ahead in early May 1939 with its own massive publicity for *The Wizard of Oz*. The campaign included postcards, posters, advertising buttons, fan club initiatives, and innumerable feature articles and images of the production placed in newspapers and magazines across the United States. The public heard its music, including "Over the Rainbow," on the *Good News* radio show of June 29, 1939.

Good News, a program that aired weekly between 1937 and 1940, was sponsored by Maxwell House and produced by MGM to showcase its own stars and films by giving listeners an auditory peek behind the scenes. The *Good News* broadcast of June 29, 1939, was devoted entirely to *The*

Wizard of Oz.[20] In segments of the show, production staff and cast members—including Garland, Ray Bolger (the Scarecrow), Bert Lahr (the Cowardly Lion), Frank Morgan (the Wizard), and the Munchkins—are heard as if in rehearsal. Some musical numbers are sung complete with a full orchestra and choir led by the regular music director of *Good News*, Meredith Willson (later to become the composer and lyricist of *The Music Man*).

"Over the Rainbow" had a prominent place in the *Good News* broadcast, which is perhaps ironic, since only weeks earlier the producers had wanted to cut it from the film. One segment of the show purported to recreate the moment when Arlen and Harburg first introduced Garland to her ballad. (Listen to example 2.4 ▶.) On the broadcast Arlen says, "Judy, we've just finished writing one of the songs you're to sing in *The Wizard of Oz*, and no one's heard it yet. So we've got our fingers crossed." "Oh, I can hardly wait," Garland replies. "Will you play it now?" After a bit more dialogue, in which Harburg tells Garland the dramatic context of the song, Arlen adds, "We try to express that yearning, the yearning of all little girls, in this song." "Sing it, Harold," Harburg commands. Arlen plays and sings the first sixteen measures (AA) in his characteristically lilting high baritone voice. Garland, excited, says she finds the song "beautiful" and "can hardly wait to learn it." "Will you teach it to me please, now?" she asks. Then, with Arlen as accompanist, she sings the A section, after which the broadcast moves on to other parts of the film.

Later in the show, the announcer Robert Young (who would go on to star in the TV series *Father Knows Best*) asks listeners to imagine themselves "on Stage 30 of the

Metro-Goldwyn-Mayer lot in the shadow of beautiful Emerald City, where scenes of *The Wizard of Oz* were made. Here in this beautiful setting, Judy Garland entertains our guests by singing her big song in the picture, 'Over the Rainbow'." And for the first time the general public heard Garland sing the song complete, with Willson's arrangement of the orchestral accompaniment. (Listen to example 2.5 ▶.) After Garland completes the song (with no coda), a chorus enters singing the second A section, after which Garland returns with the bridge and the final A section and the coda. Garland makes an error the first time through the final A section; she begins to sing "Skies are blue," rather than "Bluebirds fly," but catches her herself on "sk-" and quickly substitutes the correct words.

It is not surprising that Garland might flub a lyric. By the time of this broadcast in June 1939, she had probably not sung "Over the Rainbow" for some time, perhaps not since the filming of the Kansas scene with Vidor in February. Since early May Garland had been working nonstop on her next MGM film, *Babes in Arms*. She was on the *Babes in Arms* set the day before the *Good News* broadcast and returned to it the day after.[21]

The *Good News* broadcast was the official launch for the *Oz* music. Having tried to keep it under wraps for many months, MGM and Feist began energetically promoting the songs. Prepublication copies of the sheet music had been sent to prominent bandleaders and singers, and the official piano-vocal scores for six numbers, with cover drawings of the main characters by Al Hirschfeld, soon became available for purchase (figure 2.3). Other recorded versions of "Over the Rainbow" quickly joined those of Larry Clinton and Bea Wain, who had so egregiously jumped the

FIGURE 2.3 Original sheet music cover of "Over the Rainbow" (Summer 1939), with illustrations by Al Hirschfeld

gun back in December 1938. These included Del Courtney and vocalist Sherman Hayes (recorded July 7, 1939), Glenn Miller and Ray Eberle (July 12), and Bob Crosby and Teddy Grace (July 24).[22]

At this point, just before the release and dissemination of *The Wizard of Oz*, "Over the Rainbow" had not yet assumed an indelible association with Judy Garland; it was still (to quote Bea Wain again) just another "pretty song" that appealed to singers and bandleaders. But Garland and her managers saw the opportunity. In mid-July she signed a new one-year contract with Decca Records. On July 28, accompanied by Victor Young and his Orchestra, she recorded "Over the Rainbow" and "The Jitterbug" (now cut from *The Wizard of Oz*), the same pairing featured by Clinton. The Young-Garland versions were released in September on two sides of a 78-rpm disk. In March 1940, this disk would in turn be included with two others in the Decca album of songs from the film.

The Miller-Eberle, Crosby-Grace, and Young-Garland recordings of "Over the Rainbow" all sat at the top of the charts (numbers 1, 2, and 5, respectively) for many weeks in the fall of 1939. The Clinton-Wain recording, which had not garnered much attention on its initial appearance, rose with this tide, cresting at number 10.[23] On February 29, 1940, at the Academy Awards, "Over the Rainbow" won the Oscar for Best Song. It was well on its way to becoming the song of the century.

CHAPTER 3

HEARING THE RAINBOW

"OVER THE RAINBOW" has a structure that by the 1930s had become standard for American popular song. A "verse" or introduction of variable length (here twenty measures) sets out a broader narrative or emotional context for the number. There follows a thirty-two bar "chorus" which delivers the main expressive and melodic content, the tune we all remember. The music of the chorus is divided into four segments of eight measures each, in the form AABA. The composer presents a melody and then repeats it to anchor it in the listener's ear (AA). After a contrasting melody (B)—the ear is ready for a change—the opening segment returns exactly (A) or somewhat modified (A′) to bring the song to a close.

Structural repetition is built into the music, as described here, but the lyrics tend to change for each segment of the form, while still retaining some elements—a key word or phrase—to assure continuity and logic. The AABA form thus allows for coherence and variety, the expected and the unexpected. Composers and lyricists of the Great American Songbook, from Irving Berlin through Stephen Sondheim, worked imaginatively within this design (and some slight variants of it) in countless ways. "Over the Rainbow" is a masterwork of the form, as well as a perfectly calibrated musico-dramatic moment within *The Wizard of Oz*.

Its overall structure is:

Piano introduction (4 measures)
Verse (20 measures)
Chorus or refrain (32 measures plus coda):
  A (8 measures)
  A (8 measures)
  B ("bridge," 8 measures)
  A (8 measures)
Coda (8 measures = 4 measures instrumental, 4 vocal)

The verse was added to "Over the Rainbow" in the summer of 1938, after the completion of the chorus, to replace the spoken passages from the screenplay and to prepare the song for publication and independent performance.

In discussing the music for "Over the Rainbow" in some detail, I make the assumption that the piano-vocal score as published in the summer of 1939 represents in a meaningful sense Arlen's composition, that is, his fully realized conception of the song. Song composers differed widely in the degree to which they could or might notate their music. Some just jotted down melodies, and then arrangers filled in the harmony and accompaniment; others created relatively complete piano-vocal scores. We have very few scores in Arlen's own hand, but as suggested in chapter 1, what Sam Messenheimer apparently "transcribed" from his playing is very complete.

Arlen was notable among songwriters for his deep musicianship, which developed through his early experience as an arranger, singer, and pianist for jazz bands. The richness of his music has been recognized and admired by a number of commentators. Alec Wilder claims that Arlen's songs manifest "a greater musical thoroughness than those of other writers." "By 'thoroughness'," he clarifies, "I mean the sense of a finished product."[1] In a similar vein, Ray Bolger, a close friend of the composer who appeared in *Life Begins at 8:40* and as the Scarecrow in *The Wizard of Oz*, commented to Arlen's biographer Jablonski: "Maybe because he had been an arranger, Harold could write the song complete, with all the wonderful musical ideas written in—so that no arranger was really required."[2] Of course, once the score was out of Arlen's hands, other arrangers would make adjustments in the harmony and voice leading, as did Murray Cutter for the film soundtrack and Victor Young for Garland's Decca release.

Arlen accompanied and sang his own songs on many recordings and in numerous television and radio appearances. Most of the time, including on "Over the Rainbow," the core of his playing corresponds to the piano-vocal score, including the intricate inner parts. We can thus be confident that the published score captures Arlen's compositional vision with considerable precision, although as a pianist with deep jazz experience, he liked to improvise melodic embellishments and harmonic substitutions (as we will see in chapter 5).

THE VERSE

Regrettably, the verse of "Over the Rainbow" is rarely performed. Only one rendition appears to survive among Garland's many recorded performances of the song, from a radio broadcast of 1948. Ella Fitzgerald is one of the few major vocalists to have sung the verse. But Arlen himself clearly valued it; he sang it with enthusiasm and passion on his Capitol recording of 1955, *Harold Arlen and His Songs* (Listen to example 3.1 ▶.)

In the verse of "Over the Rainbow" Arlen and Harburg anticipate elements of both the music and lyrics of the upcoming chorus. The verse describes the world as a "hopeless jumble" in which "raindrops tumble all around." These are the rain and "dark clouds" that precede—indeed, are preconditions for—the appearance of the rainbow. Where the lyrics of the chorus emphasize flight beyond the rainbow, the verse imagines a more linear kind of transport, a "magic lane" and a "rainbow highway" that are opened up after the storm. (Perhaps Harburg's sojourn in southern California while working on *The Wizard of Oz* inspired these road-oriented images.) The message of the verse seems to be that in our imaginations, and in Dorothy's, we must stay close to the ground before we can soar over the rainbow.

The piano introduction and first four measures of the verse, with eighth-note motion and an E♭ pedal, anticipate the B section of the chorus. The latter part of the verse, from “Leading from your window pane,” relates more clearly to the A section of the chorus. The note values are longer, the harmony is more chromatic, and the melody features a large upward leap of an octave from E♭, exactly the same interval that opens the chorus at “Somewhere.” The verse also anticipates more broadly the chord progression underpinning the chorus’s opening octave leap, moving from E-flat major to C minor. The first half of the verse begins and ends in the key of E flat. The first phrase of the second half prepares a modulation to C minor (“found”), and the next phrase begins in C minor (“Leading”), which then moves back to the dominant to prepare the chorus: vi–IV–V^7.

With melodic figures that climb steeply—first an ascent of a minor seventh from C to B♭ (“To a place behind the sun”), then an eleventh from C to the high F (“Just a step beyond the rain”)—the last five measures of the verse anticipate both the melodic climax of the chorus (the F on “where you’ll *find* me”) and its coda, where the voice rises to the high E♭ on “why can’t *I*.” In the final two measures of the verse, over the dominant harmony, the right hand of the piano continues to rise past the F of the vocal part in a series of two-note chords that ascend to a high G three octaves above middle C, a note and register that are reached again only in the last measure of the chorus. In these ways Arlen and Harburg were able to make the verse an integral part of the message and the trajectory of the song as a whole.

THE CHORUS AND CODA

The chorus of “Over the Rainbow” begins with an upward octave leap on the first word, “Somewhere.” The melodic motive created by this leap and the subsequent fall of a half step (on "ov-" of "over") resembles the opening of the earliest song Arlen and Harburg wrote for *The Wizard of Oz*, "The Jitterbug," which was later cut from the film (see example 1.2). Had "Jitterbug" remained, it would have served as a kind of musical foil to "Over the Rainbow." In the ballad, the octave leap is placed firmly on strong beats, capturing Dorothy's steadfast longing for a brighter future. In the jazz dance number "The Jitterbug," the octave leap is placed on the upbeat, while the downward half step ("Who's that *hid*-ing") is placed on the first downbeat. Dorothy and her companions are living very much in the moment, trying to fend off the buzzing creatures.

The opening octave leap, something of an Arlen trademark, is especially striking when the composer alters the underlying harmony between the two notes, as he does in "Over the Rainbow," "Paper Moon" and "This Time the Dream's On Me." In "Over the Rainbow" the harmony moves from the tonic E♭ (I) to a C-minor seventh chord (vi^7). As we will see in chapter 5, jazz pianists often reharmonize the octave leap in imaginative ways to make a still greater contrast between the notes.

Across the two balanced four-measure phrases that comprise the A section of "Over the Rainbow," Arlen follows the octave leap with a gradual melodic descent back to the initial low E♭, which is reached on the "-by" of "lullaby" (example 3.1). The music presents an analogue to the arc of a rainbow, an image Arlen would have had in mind from his preliminary discussions with Harburg, even before the lyrics were fleshed out.

EXAMPLE 3.1 Octave descent across first eight measures of "Over the Rainbow"

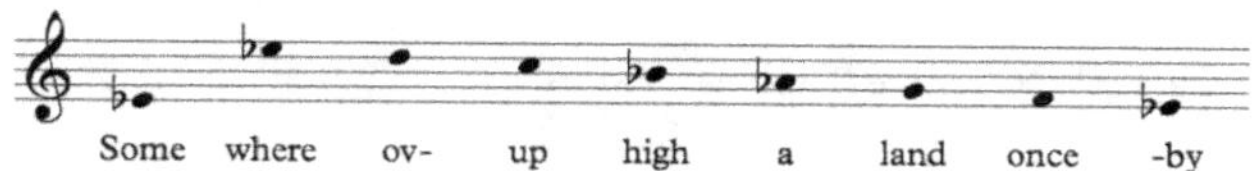

With the opening progression of "Over the Rainbow," moving from a pure major triad to a more complex minor chord, Arlen also captures the uneasy blend of hope and anxiety that lies at the core of Dorothy's personality. To some degree, Harburg works against this light-to-dark harmonic trajectory with his opening word, "Somewhere," in which a somber sound and closed vowel on "Some-" is followed by the brighter, more open "-where." But the apparent conflict between words and music only adds to the poignancy of the first measure of the song.

The two opening chords form part of a progression that, though leading quickly away from the tonic across the first two measures, moves back to it across the next two ("way up high") via a subdominant chord (IV–I) (example 3.2). This progression is a version of a so-called plagal cadence, which approaches the tonic smoothly from a consonant chord instead of from the dissonant dominant seventh found in a "perfect" cadence. A plagal cadence often appears in sacred hymns or songs at the final words "Amen"; here it reflects the prayerful tone of Dorothy's plea to escape. Arlen enhances the progression with a chromatically descending inner part in the right hand (G–G♭–F–E♭–D–D♮–C), which the left hand joins in parallel motion. Because we are only in the fourth measure, just midway through the first A section, the cadence on the word "high" is made to a first-inversion tonic chord with a G in the bass, rather than to a triad in root position, which would represent too strong a close at this point in the song.

EXAMPLE 3.2 "Over the Rainbow," chorus, mm. 3–4

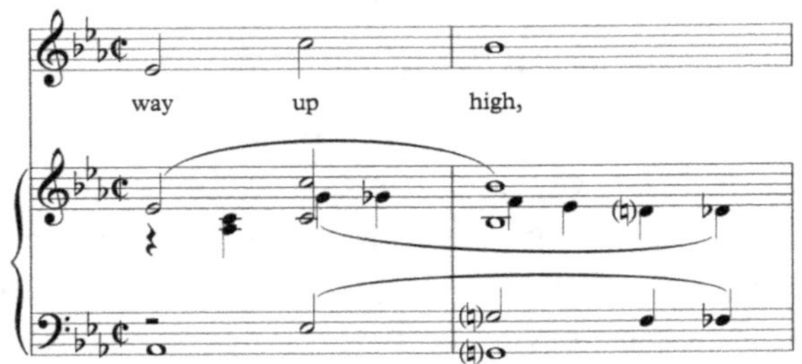

In the second four-measure phrase, Arlen intensifies the harmonic activity with chromatic alterations that are, as in measures 3–4, the result of the linear motion of the parts. Now the bass line, which had been relatively quiet, rises stepwise from the A♭ of measure 5 ("There's a") through B♭ to the C of measure 6 ("heard of"). On the "a" of "There's a," the A♭ chord is darkened to a minor triad with an added sixth. On the downbeat of the next measure ("land") we arrive on a tonic E♭ harmony with the dominant note B♭ in the bass (example 3.3). This is what is commonly called a cadential $^6_4$ chord, because the top notes are a sixth and a fourth respectively above the bass. In most cases this unstable chord resolves via the dominant harmony to the tonic in root position. But as he did when approaching the tonic in measure 4 ("up high"), Arlen thwarts that expectation; it is still too soon for full tonal closure. The bass line continues to rise, from the B♭ to C, which supports another rich harmony, a C ninth ("heard of"). Only now does Arlen initiate an extended progression moving through a circle of fifths,

C–F–B♭–E♭, the most powerful cadential gesture available in tonal music. Coming at the endpoint of this progression, the resolution of both harmony and melody to the tonic E♭ (on "-by" of "lullaby") in measure 8 feels like a genuine arrival.

EXAMPLE 3.3 "Over the Rainbow," chorus, m. 6

Although perfectly balanced, the two four-measure phrases of the A section are asymmetrical in ways that keep our ears alert and sensitive to the complexities of Dorothy's character. In the first phrase, the paired half notes on "somewhere" and "way up" make for a direct rhythmic-melodic parallel between measures 1 and 3. But in the second phrase, the parallel comes between adjacent measures, 6 and 7, each having the pattern of a quarter note followed by two eighth notes and two quarters ("land that I heard of" = "once in a lulla-").

As is common in popular songs, the second A section of "Over the Rainbow" repeats the music of the first exactly. Here, in what is a somewhat less frequent practice, Harburg also repeats the first words "Somewhere over the rainbow." The unhappy Dorothy is fixated on that image, which now yields other ideas of what lies beyond the rainbow: blue skies and fulfilled dreams. "Dream" is not the easiest word to sing, with its consonant cluster on "dr" and closed final sound on "m." The plural form "dreams" has two consonant clusters, "dr" and "ms," which constrict the sound even more. It was thus both bold and inspired for Harburg to repeat the word—and reinforce the threefold alliteration of "d" sounds—in the phrase "dreams that you dare to dream."

The B section begins in the tonic E flat, an unusual practice in the popular song repertory. Dorothy is still rooted in Kansas. Arlen pulls back from the harmonic richness of A: oscillating eighth notes in the right hand and voice (example 3.4) are supported by a five-measure E♭ pedal point in the bass. As noted earlier, Arlen claimed to have based the bridge section on the sound of a child's piano exercise. But this style captures only one side of Dorothy. While the second phrase of the bridge begins like the first—the music for "Where troubles melt like lemon drops" is identical to that for "Someday I'll wish upon a star"—for the last four measures Arlen abandons the childlike material for the chromatic style of the A section. Here we get a long descending inner line similar to what we heard in measures 3–4 (beginning at "chimney tops," F–E♭–D–C–B♭–A–A♭–G), which leads us smoothly back to the return of A (example 3.5).

EXAMPLE 3.4 "Over the Rainbow," B section (bridge), m. 17

EXAMPLE 3.5 "Over the Rainbow," end of B, mm. 23–25

Arlen also strikingly extends the melody of this second phrase. Although the total number of measures is the same in both phrases of the bridge (four), Arlen expands the final two half notes of the second phrase to four. Since the creation of the music preceded the lyrics, Harburg had to fill out those notes with extra syllables: thus "behind me" becomes "where you'll find me." A chromatic intensification of the harmony propels this melodic extension from below as the voice rises to its highest note, F ("find") above the E♭, to create the stunning climax of the song.

The third A, or reprise, of "Over the Rainbow" contains no musical surprises, but Dorothy's poetic imagination continues to develop. The "blue" of "skies are blue" from the second A section, together with the bridge's idea of soaring beyond the clouds, now stimulate in her mind the image of bluebirds. With the question "why then, oh why can't I?" she compares her own capacities with theirs. That question is important enough—indeed, it is the crux of the song—that she repeats it in the coda.

The first four measures of the coda consist of the accompaniment from the first phrase of the bridge. This practice of beginning a coda with a purely instrumental phrase is distinctive, perhaps unique, in popular song of this era. Dorothy appears to be lost in thought, momentarily unable to sing; in her mind she has perhaps already traveled to the other side of the rainbow. Then she resumes with a modified version of the bridge's melody to which are fitted lyrics adapted from the second A section ("If happy little bluebirds fly . . . why oh why can't I").

But where the second A had fallen to the low E♭, tracing the same the melodic trajectory as the other A segments, the coda's line rises to the high E♭ (example 3.6). At this final note, where she ends with a question, not a statement, we understand why the song could not have closed at the end of the last A section: the coda was necessary to "correct" the low E♭ and carry it upward to the higher octave.

EXAMPLE 3.6 "Over the Rainbow," coda, mm. 38–39

"OVER THE RAINBOW" ORCHESTRATED

We owe the luminous orchestral backdrop for "Over the Rainbow" in *The Wizard of Oz*, as recorded on October 7, 1938, to Herbert Stothart, the musical director and conductor who composed the introduction, and to Murray Cutter, a member of the MGM music staff who scored most of the numbers in the film. Arlen and Harburg had nothing directly to do with this aspect of "Over the Rainbow." Their contract with MGM for the film had ended months earlier, in August 1938. Yet this contribution of Stothart and Cutter forms an essential part of the identity of the song as experienced across generations by the countless viewers of the film or listeners to its soundtrack.

In the late 1960s MGM infamously dumped the original orchestral materials for *The Wizard of Oz* score (and for most of their classic musicals) into a landfill in Los Angeles. But working directly from the soundtrack and from some surviving musical documents, in the mid-2000s the British conductor and arranger John Wilson reconstructed the entire score, getting us probably as close to Cutter's original orchestration as is possible.[3]

Cutter (1902–83) was born in France, where he worked as a pianist in popular and concert orchestras before coming to the United States in the late 1920s. His scoring of "Over the Rainbow," with its washes of sound and the prominence of harp and celesta, strongly reflects the impressionist aesthetic of Claude Debussy and especially Maurice Ravel. Cutter told Harmetz that his orchestration of the song was "as pretty as I could make it, lots of strings and a touch of woodwind."[4]

Because Garland sang "Over the Rainbow" in the key of A flat, a fifth below the key in which it had been composed, all the materials for the soundtrack are recorded in A flat. Stothart composed the eleven-measure introduction, for which a short, or reduced, score survives, in April 1939, during the final stages of production, many months after Garland's pre-recording of October 7, 1938. It serves as underscoring for the words spoken by Dorothy to lead into the chorus of "Over the Rainbow" ("Somewhere where there isn't any trouble.").[5] (Listen to example 3.2 ▶.) From the oscillating eighth-note motion of Arlen's bridge ("Someday I'll wish upon a star") Stothart crafts a background figure played by strings and low woodwinds.

This underpins two successive melodic ideas that subtly prepare but do not directly anticipate the main tune of the song (example 3.7). First there is a yearning four-measure theme, marked by Stothart to be played "quaintly." It begins with a kind of question in the high violins, which is answered with gentle assurance by the low strings. The initial melodic motion across scale degrees 5–4–2–1 (marked in example 3.7) seems to allude to the final notes of the Bishop song "Home! Sweet Home!" (scale degrees 4–2–1 at "no place like home"), which as we have seen was an early source of inspiration for Dorothy's Kansas song and appears on several occasions in the background score of the film.[6]

EXAMPLE 3.7 Herbert Stothart, introduction to "Over the Rainbow"

In the short score Stothart labels his second melody, played by oboe and celesta, a "nursery rhyme" (at 0:11). No source has been definitively identified for this melody; Stothart may well have invented it or constructed it from a composite of songs remembered from childhood. The opening phrase seems closest to two nineteenth-century tunes, the minstrel song "Miss Lucy Long" and a version of the children's song "Round and Round the Village" (example 3.8).[7] Whatever its origin, Stothart's tune grows logically from the preceding melody.

EXAMPLE 3.8 Possible sources for Stothart's "Nursery Rhyme"

In the final three measures of the introduction (0:23) Stothart changes the meter from common time ($\frac{4}{4}$, marked 𝄴) to alla breve (𝄵), the actual meter of the rest the song. The background eighth notes become murmuring string triplets, and the main beats are marked by chords that alternate between the harp and the celesta and flutes. This pattern of marking the beats continues into the first A section of the chorus (0:31), where the main melody, sung by Garland, is accompanied by sustained chords in the low woodwinds and low strings.

For all the smoothness of the transition, the soundtrack reveals a disjunction between the introduction and chorus. Stothart conducts the introduction at an average tempo of ♩ = 70, well below the prevailing ♩ = 88 of the chorus sung by Garland. We probably owe the disparity to the fact that the introduction was recorded more than six months after the chorus; the two recordings were spliced together in later mixing. The final version of the chorus is itself a composite of several different takes, and Stothart and Garland experimented with different tempi. At the end of one of the outtakes we hear Stothart ask her: "Want another one like this, then a fast one?"[8]

For the second A section (0:53), Cutter brings in the violins with a new countermelody based on the rising sixth motive of "way up." In the B section, the high strings drop out at first, and the vocal melody is shadowed by three flutes playing full triads in parallel motion, while an alto clarinet in low (or *chalumeau*) register plays the countermelody that in Arlen's piano version is in the top of the left hand. The high strings are absent at first but provide a gentle stepwise rejoinder in between phrases and then return at the climax, with "where you'll find me." In the final A section, at "bluebirds fly," the first violins flutter up and down chromatically in parallel triads.

Cutter continues to work his magic in the coda (beginning at 2:09). During the purely instrumental portion, supplemented unforgettably by bird calls, the melody is again played in parallel motion by three flutes, while the alto clarinet resumes its haunting obbligato; high strings flutter with soft tremolos; the celesta plays arpeggiated chords; and the harp sustains the dominant E♭ pedal point in sweeping glissandi. On the sustained "I," the final word of the song, there appear the murmuring triplets that Stothart would foreshadow in his introduction, and the harp and violas play a rising figure in quarter notes that is an augmented version of Arlen's original.

"Over the Rainbow" has been arranged countless times since 1939, but perhaps no later version has ever captured the original spirit of the song, especially its chiaroscuro of hope and sadness, better than that created by Stothart and Cutter for the soundtrack.

CHAPTER 4

A GARLAND OF RAINBOWS

ABOVE THE TITLE ON the first page of the sheet music as published in the summer of 1939 by Leo Feist, Inc., is a line in small italic type: *Sung by Dorothy**. Following the asterisk to the bottom of the page, we read, in the same small type, **Dorothy—Judy Garland.* Such indications were fairly common in sheet music for songs from Hollywood and Broadway. But read today, it can seem an egregious understatement. No other American popular song has become so indelibly linked with a singer—and with that singer as a character—as has "Over the Rainbow" with Garland in the role of Dorothy Gale. We associate "White Christmas" with Bing Crosby and "My Way" with Frank Sinatra. But "Over the Rainbow," Garland, and Dorothy have a unique triangular relationship that has endured for almost eighty years.

"OVER THE RAINBOW" IN GARLAND'S CAREER

Garland acknowledged, and mostly embraced, this association with "Over the Rainbow." In 1961 she told Arlen's biographer Jablonski:

> [As for] my feeling toward "Over the Rainbow" now, it has become a part of my life. It is so symbolic of everybody's dream and wish that I am sure that's why people sometimes get tears in their eyes when they hear it. I have sung it dozens of times and it's still the song that is closest to my heart. It is very gratifying to have a song that is more or less known as my song, or my theme song, and to have had it written by the fantastic Harold Arlen.[1]

"Over the Rainbow" captured not only the innocence of the teenage Dorothy but also the tumult of Garland's adulthood, which was marked by substance abuse, depression, weight problems, hospitalizations, failed marriages, custody battles, and financial difficulties. Even the straight-laced *New York Times* wrote, in Garland's obituary of June 1969: "Miss Garland's personal life often seemed a fruitless search for the happiness promised in 'Over the Rainbow.' "[2]

Garland would sometimes dismiss such claims. In 1960 she noted, with humor: "I've discovered that part of the wonderful richness of the world lies in its imperfections. That land that lies over the rainbow is probably a terrible bore to live in, anyhow."[3] Garland could also chafe at being yoked so often to the character of the teenage Dorothy from *The Wizard of Oz*. In 1960, when Queen Elizabeth the Queen Mother remarked how moved she always was by "Over the Rainbow," Garland politely quipped, "Ma'am, that song has plagued me throughout the years. It's like being a grandmother in pigtails" (5).

Garland sang "Over the Rainbow" throughout her career.[4] Yet it took time to become her "theme" song. *The Wizard of Oz* was not seen with any frequency until regular television broadcasts began in the late 1950s. Although Garland's studio recording for Decca in July 1939 was a big success, other songs from her film work at MGM dominated charts for a while, including "The Trolley Song," "On the Atchison, Topeka and the Santa Fe," and "Zing! Went the Strings of My Heart." During the 1940s "Over the Rainbow" began to eclipse them in her regular repertory, and by the 1950s it became paramount as the much-awaited climax of her many concert appearances.

Early on, Garland willingly participated in parodies of "Over the Rainbow." On October 8, 1944, at a dinner for the Hollywood Democratic Committee, accompanied by Johnny Green at the piano, she sang a version in which the A section had appropriately ill-fitting lyrics (Listen to example 4.1 ▶):

The Democratic Committee
Loves you so.
You're cute, you're smart, and you're pretty,
Also we need your dough.[5]

A few months later, on February 15, 1945, Garland took part in an Armed Forces Radio Service radio broadcast for overseas troops. This was a fifty-five-minute show called *Dick Tracy in B-Flat*, billed by the announcer as "the first comic strip operetta."[6] With music arranged by Meredith Willson, it featured some of the most famous actors and recording stars of the day, including Crosby, Sinatra, Bob Hope, Dinah Shore, Jimmy Durante, and Garland's erstwhile *Oz* costar Frank Morgan. In *Dick Tracy in B-Flat* Garland plays a character named Snowflake Falls, who is held captive by the villainous Flattop (Bob Hope). (Listen to example 4.2 ▶.) She sings the A section of "Over the Rainbow" with the words

> Somewhere over a barrel,
> Black and blue,
> Smiling bravely the while
> I wait for a music cue.

Immediately after this, Garland breaks into a parody of the main theme of the sextet from Donizetti's opera *Lucia di Lammermoor.*

Starting in the 1950s, as she became more personally identified with the song, Garland resisted doing any parodic versions. Mel Tormé, the musical supervisor for her television series *The Judy Garland Show*, which ran during the 1963–64 season, recalled that he and his staff had proposed to Garland "doing a rather funny bit built around 'Over the Rainbow.'" She stared at them in astonishment.

> "You've got to be kidding," she said sternly.
> "Uh . . . no . . . no Judy, we thought it would be pretty funny if—"

> "There will be *no* jokes of any kind about 'Over the Rainbow'!" she said evenly. "It's kind of . . . sacred. I don't want anybody *anywhere* to lose the thing they have about Dorothy or that song!"[7]

Garland sang "Over the Rainbow" only once in the twenty-six episodes of *The Judy Garland Show*, at the very end of the Christmas special that was broadcast December 22, 1963. (View example 4.3 ▶.) After a holiday medley, and when all the revelers have left her stage "home," Judy begins to wrap up the show. As she turns off the stage lights, her real-life children Lorna and Joey Luft come out in their bathrobes and say, "Mama, you forgot something! You know, the thing you do every year!" Garland takes them over to the sofa, and with one child on either side—and with many hugs and kisses in between the phrases—sings "Over the Rainbow." Here the song has indeed become "sacred," an ersatz Christmas carol of love and hope.

Garland would usually conclude her live concerts with "Over the Rainbow," which was then followed by one or more faster encores. At her first major concert with orchestra, at Robin Hood Dell in Philadelphia, on July 1, 1943, an event that drew over thirty thousand spectators, Garland ended her second medley with "Over the Rainbow," before closing the show with the "The Joint Is Really Jumping Down at Carnegie Hall," a rousing number by Roger Edens, Hugh Martin, and Ralph Blane.[8] This pattern continued in many of her performances during the 1950s and 1960s. Even though she clearly rehearsed and planned to sing "Over the Rainbow," it became something that audiences had to beg for, a first encore rather than the last programmed number.

Garland and her producers modified this strategy to great dramatic effect in her legendary engagement at the Palace Theater in New York, which extended from October 1951 to February 1952. Here, and in programs modeled on it, she sang "Over the Rainbow" as the very last number. Although the Palace shows were not filmed, Garland recreated much of their content for the *Ford Star Jubilee* television broadcast of September 24, 1955.[9] "Over the Rainbow" follows the Irving Berlin dance number "A Couple of Swells," which Garland and Fred Astaire, dressed in tramp costumes, had originally sung in the movie *Easter Parade* (1948). In concert, Garland, outfitted with a dilapidated top hat and her face smudged with make-believe stubble, would perform "A Couple of Swells" with a partner (no longer Astaire). At its conclusion she would come forward, sit alone with her legs hanging over the edge of the stage, a spotlight focused on her face, and sing "Over the Rainbow" (figure 4.1). (View example 4.4 ▶.)

This placement of "Over the Rainbow" in the Palace show definitively inverts the narrative of *The Wizard of Oz*, and in doing so alters the meaning of the song. "Over the Rainbow" appeared near the beginning of the film as an expression of the young Dorothy's sense of hope and longing. Coming near the end of the Palace show, "Over the Rainbow" captures a more mature, world-wearier Garland, hopeful but also realistic.

Garland deployed "Over the Rainbow" to tremendous effect in her renowned Carnegie Hall concert of April 23, 1961, which was recorded in full and released on a Grammy-winning double album.[10] The song appears in the orchestral overture but then is not heard again for almost two hours. The official program ends with Garland's rousing version

FIGURE 4.1 Judy Garland as the Tramp singing "Over the Rainbow" (1955)

of "Rock-a-Bye Your Baby With a Dixie Melody." During the extended applause, as she takes her bows, the orchestra plays the entire chorus of "Over the Rainbow," minus the coda. After the music dies down, Garland says to her audience, "I know.... I'll sing 'em all, and we'll stay all night," a comment greeted with enormous cheers. "I don't ever want to go home," she adds, and then without any further orchestral introduction begins to sing "Over the Rainbow." (Listen to example 4.5 ▶.) Having withheld the song throughout the concert, she finally gives it to her audience. She follows "Over the Rainbow" with three more encores, "Swanee," "After You've Gone," and "Chicago."

SOME GARLAND "RAINBOWS"

For all the fandom surrounding Garland, few commentators have analyzed closely the singing of one of the great vocal artists of the twentieth century. Garland's theme song, "Over the Rainbow," which she sang both live and in the studio, offers such an opportunity. Live, she was magical and charismatic. When singing "Over the Rainbow" at or near the very end of her shows, she was audibly fatigued. Yet in the 1955 television broadcast, after dancing in "A Couple of Swells," Garland uses her shortness of breath to powerful effect at the final words "why oh why can't I" in the coda. This catch in the throat, sometimes resembling a sob or large sigh, became one of her most distinctive expressive devices.

The studio offered Garland a venue for performances that show her technique and expressive skills to best advantage, without any significant loss of the spontaneous intensity that is her hallmark. Five of Garland's performances of "Over the Rainbow" can be considered true studio recordings; with no live audience, they were made under conditions that (at least in principle) allowed for retakes:

- October 7, 1938: the soundtrack recording for *The Wizard of Oz*, with orchestration by Murray Cutter, conducted by Hebert Stothart
- July 28, 1939: her first commercial release of the song, on Decca, with Victor Young and his Orchestra
- August 13, 1944: a so-called V-disc, with Tommy Dorsey and his orchestra (V-discs—V is for "victory"—were produced during World War II for military personnel overseas)
- August 25, 1955: her first of two recordings with orchestra for Capitol Records, conducted by Jack Cathcart, released on the LP *Miss Show Business* (1955)

- August 4, 1960: the second Capitol recording, made in London, conducted by Norrie Paramor, released in 1972 on the LP *Judy in London*

Garland tended to sing only the chorus of "Over the Rainbow"; there is a single recorded example of her performing the verse, on the Louella Parsons Show in December 1948. And she always sang "Over the Rainbow" in the key of A flat, a fifth below Arlen's notated E flat, a key well suited to her contralto range.

In these studio recordings made over twenty-two years, many aspects of Garland's interpretation change significantly, including tempo, timbre, rhythm, phrasing, diction, and choice of pitches. In general, and not surprisingly, the recordings move from a stricter adherence to Arlen's notated melody to a much freer approach. These expressive differences mirror the trajectory of Garland's own personal and professional life, a shift from Dorothy Gale to Judy Garland as "author" of the song. But even a listener not familiar with *The Wizard of Oz* or Garland's biography will experience the earlier recordings as meltingly touching and the later ones as emotionally devastating.

The earliest versions are also the fastest. The soundtrack version unfolds at about ♩ = 88; the Decca recording is a shade faster at 90. Both conform in spirit to the "foxtrot ballad," a characteristic designation of the era for any number in moderate tempo and duple meter, and a label applied to "Over the Rainbow" by the MGM music department in an internal memo of 1938.[11] Only later did Garland and other singers transform it into more of a torch song, which is characterized by melancholy expression of unrequited desire.

The soundtrack recording captures Garland's hallmark blend of purity and richness, of focus and nuance. (Listen to example 4.6 ▶.) Although she stays close to Arlen's notated pitches, except for the short trill on "blue" of "Skies are blue" (a gesture she would drop later on), Garland phrases his melody with great fluidity and expression. In this, as in so many other ways, she channels Dorothy, in whom impulses toward obedience and independence compete.

Garland performs the first phrase on a single breath, as a continuous upward arc, like the rainbow about which she is singing. The first syllable ("Some-") is soft and covered, almost hesitant. The bold upward octave leap to "-where" thus becomes a surprise. Garland avoids a distinct articulation of the initial "wh-" aspirate of the word "where," in order to push smoothly, with the tiniest bit of a slide or glissando, toward the vowel and the brighter "-ere." She darkens her voice with the next word "over" by bringing the "v" closer to the "o" than the notation and text underlay ("o-ver") would suggest. She also lingers on that syllable a fraction longer than the notated quarter note, before resuming a steadier rhythm with the following syllables, "-er" and "the." The quarter notes of "rainbow"—the central image of the song—are held out somewhat longer than their notated value.

Garland delays the downbeat on "land" in measure 6 by a fraction of a beat, and then articulates the "l" clearly and distinctly, thereby placing appropriate emphasis on the important tonic $^{6}_{4}$ chord discussed in chapter 3. As with "over" in the rhythmically and melodically parallel spot in measure 2, she holds "land" longer than its notated quarter note but resumes stricter rhythm on "that I heard of." Then a pause and a breath, which brings in "once" just after the downbeat of measure 7 such that it sounds syncopated. Like "rainbow" in measure 2, "lullaby" is notated in even quarter notes. But Garland shortens the first syllable to about an eighth note and extends the second to a dotted quarter, so that syncopation is felt once again.

In the bridge, after holding out the "Some" of "Some day," Garland sings the oscillating eighth notes (the imitation of the child's piano exercise, as Arlen claimed) in fairly strict rhythm, slowing for the climax at "where you'll find me." The last A section is much like the earlier ones. In the coda, the eighth notes are again regular, and then Garland slows the melody and thins her voice, in what becomes a diminuendo, as she rises to the high note on "why oh why can't I?" Thus the last melodic highpoint on "I" (A♭ in Garland's version) is not so much climactic as wistful.

Garland's interpretation on the Decca recording of "Over the Rainbow," made just before the film's release, resembles the soundtrack version in many respects, but it also clearly reflects the context of the commercial studio. (Listen to example 4.7 ▶.) She was now singing as a seventeen-year-old professional vocal artist, not a twelve-year-old Kansas girl. Young's silky smooth orchestral backdrop differs considerably from Cutter's translucent one. Garland responds with a slightly faster, steadier tempo and somewhat less rhythmic fluidity.

The most striking change in Garland's Decca version involves an alteration at the opening of the last reprise of the A section, one that would define all of her later performances. As is common in many commercial song recordings with orchestra, the full chorus (AABA) is followed by an instrumental version of the A section (at 1:41), here featuring a mellow solo clarinet, which ends with a jaunty tag (1:58), suggesting how far the song already has traveled from Kansas. Garland then sings one more reprise of A (2:02) starting forte on the higher octave, so that both syllables of "Somewhere" are sung on the same pitch. She then drops in volume and makes a similar melodic change at "bluebirds" and then at "birds fly," in both cases replacing the notated upward sixth leaps with repeated notes (example 4.1).

EXAMPLE 4.1 Garland's melodic alterations of "Over the Rainbow" reprise

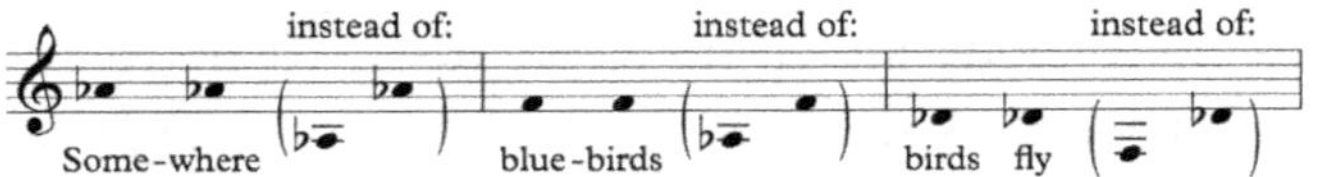

These alterations make more audible the long-range octave descent of the A melody (seen in example 3.1), providing a clear contrast or counterweight to the final rise back to the higher octave in the coda. In the Decca recording, these changes give the altered reprise more of a sense of climax than in the soundtrack. But only in later recordings would Garland turn it into something emotionally shattering. We get a preview of this approach in a powerful live concert performance that Garland did with Arlen at the piano in San Francisco in September 1940.[12] (Listen to example 4.8 ▶.)

In the mid-1950s, Garland's voice had developed a darker, grittier texture, with wider vibrato, but with a sense of pitch as secure as ever. The 1955 Capitol version of "Over the Rainbow" has a slow tempo, ♩ = 65. The 1960 version is slower still, at ♩ = 60, proportionally a third slower than the

Decca recording of 1939. (Listen to examples 4.9 and 4.10 ▶.) Along with the relaxation of tempo comes an approach to the song that is still more fluid, more confessional, and characterized at many moments by Garland's unique catch in the throat.

The narrative and musical trajectories of "Over the Rainbow" also change in the later recordings, especially the handling of the climax. When interpreting the song with greater literalness in 1938 and 1939, Garland gives expressive emphasis to the melodic highpoint, the B♭ at the end of the bridge or B section ("where you'll *find* me"), then resumes a more subdued mood for the return of the A section. In the 1955 and 1960 Capitol recordings Garland extends the climax of the song. Maintaining intensity in volume and tempo, she pushes past "find" into the beginning of the A section and through the entire return of the phrase "Somewhere over the rainbow." Only then does she drop in volume for "bluebirds fly," singing the remainder of the A section quietly, almost resignedly. At the end of the coda, for "Why oh why can't I," where in 1938 and '39 she softens the volume, Garland now builds to a powerful second climax, emphasizing the individual words of that last phrase, as in the 1955 television performance.

In 1938 and 1939, Garland's phrasing and breathing closely track the song's natural units. In 1955 Garland divides the opening phrase "Somewhere over the rainbow" in two, with a short glottal stop or sob after "Somewhere," as if she is first expressing the desire to be elsewhere and only then imagines a destination over the rainbow. The later Garland is still clearly capable of longer phrases. In a stunning effect, Garland in 1955 sings "There's a land that

I heard of once" on a single breath, eliding the "once" that would normally be part of the next phrase. As Dorothy in the soundtrack, the singer quite naturally links the "once" to what follows, "in a lullaby," just as it appears in Harburg's lyric and in the metrical structure of Arlen's melody. She is recalling a moment that is closer in time to her singing. On the 1955 recording, Garland is in a different temporal and emotional space. It is as if she knows that she heard of this land "once," at some moment in the past, but she cannot at first recall exactly where or when. Then, in that pause, she remembers: "in a lullaby."

Garland's Capitol recordings of "Over the Rainbow" are filled with such exquisite interpretive details. The oscillating eighth notes of the bridge, which Garland interprets more literally in 1938 and 1939, are now shaped freely, meditatively. The Capitol Garland seems to respond to the fact that while the first two A sections of the song have only one reference to "I" or "me" in sixteen measures ("land that *I* heard of"), the bridge has three within eight measures ("*I'll* wish," "behind *me*," and "find *me*"). The bridge is thus no longer the echo of a child's piano exercise, but a journey further into the singer's soul. In both the 1955 and the 1960 recordings Garland's loudest sobbing comes at "you'll," the only moment in the song where the singer turns most explicitly outward from herself to us, the listener. Garland's performance of the bridge on these later recordings prepares the song's climax in a way that is at once logical and thrilling, bursting the formal boundaries, continuing through "find me" and extending into the first full phrase of the reprise of A.

In her liner notes to the three-CD set of selections from the Garland Capitol recordings, *Judy Garland: The One and*

Only, Emily Coleman eloquently summarizes the qualities of these later "Rainbow" performances. After emphasizing the wistfulness of the 1938 soundtrack recording, she observes:

> There is nothing wistful about the Capitol versions of "Over the Rainbow." . . . "Rainbow" is now a song of haunting sadness. But it is sadness without self-pity. For Garland makes it a song of striving as well. . . . Instead of thinning her voice at the end, she uses her full vocal force, adding increasing power to each successive syllable of the last phrases, and she stresses the "can't" in "why can't I?" With the pulsating strength of vibrato, the force of the ending seems to be a cry from the heart.[13]

Garland likely was not conscious of many of the expressive nuances that Coleman identifies here and that I have discussed in detail in this chapter. For a great singer such gestures become instinctive. And yet we should not assume they are beyond (or beneath) analysis. When we examine Garland's performances of "Over the Rainbow," using our words to render what is almost ineffable, we describe not just how she interprets the song but also how that interpretation affects us as listeners. There is no clear boundary; what links Garland's performance and our response is the song "Over the Rainbow." It exists on paper in the notes and words of the piano-vocal score created by Arlen and Harburg. But the song's magic is experienced only when it traverses the distance between Garland's soul and our own, via her voice and our ears. It is that space we explore in our analysis of the performances.

GARLAND, "OVER THE RAINBOW," AND THE SOUND OF THE CLOSET

On the LGBT entertainment website *The Backlot*, the writer Steven Frank wrote in 2007: "When Judy Garland sang 'Over the Rainbow,' the sadness in her voice, even when singing about such happy images as bluebirds and lemon drops, was palpable, hinting at complex depths beyond the wholesome image projected on screen. This was, in effect, the sound of the closet, and it spoke to gay men's consciousness that the image they presented in their own public lives was often at odds with a truer sense of self that mainstream society would not condone."[14]

A year later, in Gus Van Sant's film *Milk* about the career and brutal murder of the gay San Francisco supervisor Harvey Milk, Garland's original soundtrack recording of "Over the Rainbow" accompanies historic footage from the 1978 San Francisco Gay Freedom Day Parade. We see marchers waving the Rainbow Flag, designed for the parade by Gilbert Baker. Baker has noted that in creating his flag he was not consciously inspired by Garland and "Over the Rainbow." For him, Garland's iconic status belonged to an older generation. Barbra Streisand was Baker's diva, and the Rolling Stones' "She's a Rainbow" had a more direct influence on his flag concept. Yet Baker accepts that Garland, "Over the Rainbow," and his flag have become strands of a common mythology.[15] Frank's article, the sequence from Van Sant's *Milk*, and Baker's remarks all reflect how for many decades a fourth element, gay male culture, has intersected the Dorothy-Garland-"Rainbow" triangle mentioned at the beginning of this chapter. Here we can only touch upon some of those associations.[16]

The phrase "friends of Dorothy" surfaced periodically in the last half of the twentieth century as a coded reference among gay men. The origins of this phrase are by no means clear, but most commentators believe it derives from *The Wizard of Oz*, where Dorothy's three male companions are, as Dee Michel writes, "gentle, loving, and silly."[17] The Cowardly Lion is distinctly feminized with a range of stereotypes. In Harburg's lyrics he confesses to having been born a "sissy," adding, "I'm afraid there's no denyin' / I'm just a dandy lion." He occasionally shows a limp wrist, and the top of his mane gets tied with a bow during his makeover in the Emerald City. The apparent contradiction between the lion's fearsome exterior and fearful interior resonated with some closeted men who felt they had to appear "straight." In 1998, one man told a reporter for the *Atlanta Constitution*: "In the mid-'60s there were no gay role models. I was around 11 or 12, and I just knew the lion was my role model. . . . The movie told me it was OK to be gay. The Wizard told him he didn't need to change because inside he was just as good as everyone else."[18]

During the 1950s, as Garland's concert and recording career expanded, she became a gay icon. The film scholar Richard Dyer documents the impressions and feelings of many gay men who attended Garland's concerts, watched her films, and listened to her recordings in that decade. He points out that Garland singing "Over the Rainbow" takes on "a particular resonance for the gay reading because it is of a piece with all the other aspects of her image that can be read from a gay perspective."[19] These include the categories that he identifies as "ordinariness" (the girl-next-door characters Garland played in her MGM films), "androgyny" (suggested by some of her masculine outfits), and "camp" (a sense of parody and artifice in some of her films).

According to some who shared their stories with Dyer, Garland would, especially near the end of her career, personalize "Over the Rainbow" in a way that seemed to speak directly to gay men in the audience. One reported that at a concert in Philadelphia in 1968, she said, "I finally made it over the rainbow thanks to you all." She began the song, then interrupted it by yelling, "We can all do it, you know." She then resumed the song and ended with, "Thank you. God bless you" (148).

Dyer suggests that the tramp outfit in which Garland sang "Over the Rainbow" from the front of the stage at the end of her concert performances may have held a special appeal for gay men (figure 4.1). In the films *Summer Stock* and *A Star Is Born* Garland had done some numbers (notably "Get Happy") in what Dyer calls a "vamp" style, with a fedora hat and a short suit jacket worn over very short pants and sheer stockings. Dyer describes the look as "an androgynous image with sex appeal" (173). The tramp image of "Over the Rainbow" presented something different. "If in the vamp gay men could identify with someone whose sexuality is accepted by the boys," Dyer notes, "in the tramp we could identify with someone who has left sexuality behind in an androgyny that is . . . without gender" (175–76). The idea that getting "Over the Rainbow" could mean getting beyond gender is a powerful one and points to a special aspect of the song's history.

After Garland's death in June 1969 and the Stonewall riots that followed less than a week later—her death has sometimes been identified as a precipitating factor—she appears to have faded somewhat as a gay icon, as Baker implies in his remarks quoted above. By 2000, the *Atlantic* could feature an article entitled "The Queen is Dead," with the subheading, "Once a gay icon, Judy Garland has become an embarrassment." The author, Michael Joseph Gross, explained that since gay life had become more incorporated into the mainstream culture in recent decades, "gay men in this generation are mostly indifferent to the faux tragedy and flamboyant exoticism of camp, and to old-time gay icons like Judy Garland."[20] A dozen years later, when *End of the Rainbow*, a play about Garland's final days, opened on Broadway, Robert Leleux wrote a commentary in the *New York Times* entitled "The Road Gets Rougher for Judy's Faithful," observing how some gay men could not relate to the image of Garland portrayed in the play. "Today, Judyism, like Yiddish, is little more than a cultural memory," Leleux observed.[21]

Yet one prominent and openly gay entertainer has made Judyism a central aspect of his career. In a pair of sold-out concerts in June 2006 at Carnegie Hall, which he reprised a decade later, Rufus Wainwright recreated the entirety of Garland's legendary Carnegie concert of 1961. The posters for the event directly evoke Garland's, even down to the characterization (surely somewhat tongue-in-cheek) of Wainwright as the "world's greatest entertainer" (figures 4.2a and b). In a review, the *New York Times* critic Stephen Holden observed, "What unfolded onstage was a tour de force of politically empowering performance art in which a proudly gay male performer paid homage to the original and longest-running gay icon in the crowded pantheon of pop divas."[22] An album made from Wainwright's

(a)

FIGURE 4.2 Posters for Carnegie Hall Concerts by (a) Judy Garland (1961) and (b) Rufus Wainwright (2006)

(b)

FIGURE 4.2 Continued

show, *Rufus Does Judy*, released in December 2007, earned a Grammy nomination, strong reviews, and decent sales.

"Over the Rainbow" has played an important role in Wainwright's life. As a little boy he was taught the song by his mother, the folk singer Kate McGarrigle, who called it "the best of the bunch" of "songs she would sing for solace."[23] During the early 2000s, after 9/11 and the subsequent American invasions of Afghanistan and Iraq, Wainwright listened repeatedly to Garland's double Carnegie album, which, "no matter how dark things seemed, made everything brighten." He said of Garland: "She had this capacity to lighten the world through the innocence of her sound. Her anchor to the material was obviously through her devotion to music. You never feel that she didn't believe every word of every song she ever sang."[24]

Wainwright personalized "Over the Rainbow" at Carnegie Hall in 2006. (Listen to example 4.11 ▶.) For the first A section he was accompanied by his mother on piano; only after this did the orchestra enter with the original scoring. In his very slow rendition of the song (♩ = 50) Wainwright did not mimic or channel Garland, but rather seemed to go after the sincerity and fluidity he so admired in her singing. Despite mannerisms like sliding up to high notes from just below (as on the opening "Somewhere"), Wainwright deployed what one critic has called his "dulcet foghorn of a voice" with feeling and nuance.[25] Especially effective was his move to head voice for the high note on "find" in the bridge, which contrasted with the breathy low register he used for the end of the reprise of the A section.

The applause after "Over the Rainbow," as Wainwright took his bow, seemed almost as thunderous as that which greeted Garland in 1961. This ambitious but affecting tribute to Judy Garland by one of today's most esteemed pop musicians shows that although some aspects of Judyism may be dead, her "Over the Rainbow" remains a powerful cultural force. The difference today from 1961 or even 2006, the date of Wainwright's first concert homage, is that gay culture now forms even more clearly a part of America's broader culture. Dorothy, Oz, Garland, and "Over the Rainbow" have consistently accompanied that journey.

CHAPTER 5
IVORY RAINBOWS

A DURABLE ENTRY IN the Great American Songbook as well as a jazz standard, "Over the Rainbow" has been recorded thousands of times. The Jazz Discography Online, which focuses mainly on instrumentalists and the vocalists who recorded with them, lists 1,045 versions made between the Clinton-Wain disk released in 1939 and 2017.[1] Another database, SecondHandSongs, lists 662 versions, divided into vocal and instrumental.[2] "Over the Rainbow" is number 10 among the "most covered songs" in history.[3] Along with "Summertime" (no. 1) and "Body and Soul" (no. 9), "Over the Rainbow" is one of the few top songs that is not Christmas-related.

Garland's performances of "Over the Rainbow" tend to overshadow other versions and have even discouraged many vocalists from taking it up. In a spoken introduction to a live recording of 1987, Barbra Streisand calls "Over the Rainbow" "one of the finest songs ever written" but says she resisted singing it "because it's identified with one of the greatest singers who ever lived."[4] In addition to Streisand, singers who overcame hesitation and made notable recordings of "Over the Rainbow" include Frank Sinatra (1945), Rosemary Clooney (1952), Sarah Vaughan (1956), Diahann Carroll (1957), Aretha Franklin (1960), Ella Fitzgerald (1961), Tony Bennett (1961), Patti LaBelle (1981), Eva Cassidy (1992), Jane Monheit (2004), Judy Collins (2010), and Josh Groban (2015).

Here we will focus not on singers but on jazz pianists, who provide a different but vital subset of "Over the Rainbow" interpretations. With a keyboard, ten fingers, and vast musical imaginations, these artists transform "Over the Rainbow" into miniature (and occasionally not so miniature) tone poems. In the absence of Harburg's lyrics, these artists nonetheless convey a story or a trajectory for "Over the Rainbow." They "sing" it as expressively and as meaningfully as the greatest vocalists. Their recordings are especially relevant to a study of "Over the Rainbow" because of the composer's strong affinity for jazz. Arlen began his professional career in the late 1920s as an arranger, pianist, and vocalist in several bands. Many of his songs, most famously "Stormy Weather" and others written for Harlem's Cotton Club in the early 1930s, show a deep immersion in jazz styles.

Arlen played the piano frequently on recordings and on radio and television, accompanying himself or other singers. The very first recordings of "Over the Rainbow" in which he participated were those made for the *Good News* radio broadcast of June 29, 1939, discussed in chapter 2. Although jazz elements are much scarcer in the score of "Over the Rainbow" than in many of his other songs, Arlen manages to indulge his jazz impulses at certain moments. In the staged recreation of Garland's first exposure to "Over the Rainbow" on that radio show, he improvises a one-measure lead-in based on the bridge theme (1:22) before singing and playing the first two A sections himself. (Listen to example 5.1 ▶.) As Garland prepares to sing (in the key of A flat), Arlen precedes the chorus with an insouciant bluesy measure that inflects the opening octave leap with a flatted seventh (2:25) (example 5.1).

EXAMPLE 5.1 Arlen, improvised lead-in to Garland performance of "Over the Rainbow" (1939)

Another early example of a brief Arlen improvisation is his performance with Garland at a concert in San Francisco in September 1940.[5] (Listen to example 5.2 ▶.) As an introduction Arlen plays alone through the first A section of the chorus more or less literally, but with a few harmonic enrichments; in measure 6, at the melody for "land that I heard of" (0:17) he adds a tiny chromatic ornament. Then in the piano interlude after Garland's first A section he departs more radically with a characteristic early jazz figure that slides into the dominant from a parallel chord a half step above (0:51) (example 5.2).

EXAMPLE 5.2 Arlen transitional measure between A segments (1940)

Arlen's interpolations might seem incompatible with the childlike innocence of "Over the Rainbow" as projected by Dorothy and the early Garland. But he understood that the song's rainbow could encompass many different musical colors. Indeed, jazz pianists have found "Over the Rainbow" an ideal canvas for the kinds of improvisation Arlen only hints at in his recordings.

Distinguished solo (or mainly solo) recordings of "Over the Rainbow," many captured live, include:

Art Tatum (1939, ca. 1948, 1953, 1956)
Bud Powell (1951, 1956)
George Shearing (1951, 1963)
Dave Brubeck (1952)
Ellis Larkins (1952)
Oscar Peterson (1954, 1959)
Erroll Garner (1955)
Dick Marx (1955)
André Previn (1960)
Mary Lou Williams (1978)
Keith Jarrett (1982, 1984, 1991, 1995, 2009)

We will look at some of these recordings, which refract Arlen and Harburg's song through a wide prism of jazz styles—from the stride-inflected virtuosity of Art Tatum, to the bebop intensity of Bud Powell, to the cool, fluid elegance of Dick Marx, and the harmonic and motivic intricacy of André Previn, to the meditative counterpoint of Keith Jarrett.

ART TATUM, BUD POWELL, AND ERROLL GARNER

In August 1939, almost simultaneously with the release of *The Wizard of Oz* and at a time when few were familiar with its music, Art Tatum became the first jazz pianist (and one of the first artists altogether) to record "Over the Rainbow," on a transcription disk prepared for radio broadcast. Tatum's unique artistry offered a vision of the song different not only from Garland's but also from some of the early big-band versions by figures like Larry Clinton, Glenn Miller, and Bob Crosby. Tatum would go on to release three other versions over the course of his career. Chronological priority alone would make Tatum's 1939 version worthy of attention. But more significant is its musical inventiveness, which inspired several generations of jazz pianists. (Listen to example 5.3 ▶.)

As if alerting us to the fact that we are definitely not in Kansas anymore, Tatum introduces the chorus of "Over the Rainbow" with two statements of a pungent, upward rolled dominant chord with a flatted ninth (that is, lowered by a half step) and a raised eleventh and thirteenth (thus, in the key of D, where he plays the song: A–C♯–G–B♭–D♯–F♯), punctuated by bell-like octaves in the right hand.[6] Tatum then plays three full choruses of "Over the Rainbow," each becoming progressively more virtuosic. The first (0:07) uses block chords. The second (1:17) features Tatum's distinctive swing-style adaptation of stride, bass-to-chord accompaniment. The third (2:51) begins with the swing style, but the right hand becomes ever more elaborate and the music begins to modulate widely.

Tatum tends to perform Arlen's melody mostly straight, but underpins it with a wide array of substitutions for the original harmonies. For example, on the downbeat of measure 4 ("high"), where Arlen has a simple first-inversion tonic chord (with suspension), Tatum plays a rich half-diminished chord over the original bass note, F♯ (0:12). In between phrases of "Over the Rainbow" he intersperses his trademark lightning-fast scales (sometimes impressionistic whole-tone ones) and arpeggios running up and down almost the entire length of the keyboard.

Each pianist's version of "Over the Rainbow" can be rewarding to examine for the B or bridge section alone, which as we have seen begins simply and diatonically (in the manner of a child's piano exercise, according to Arlen) before becoming more chromatic and climactic. Tatum tends to play the bridge section in a plainer style than the first chorus. But he also provides distinct contrast in its third and fourth measures by slipping magically into and then out of a kind of alternate, highly chromatic universe (at 0:41, 2:01, 3:23). By the third time the bridge comes around, it has been fully infiltrated by arrays of dissonant notes, providing a climax to the entire performance before a brief, almost perfunctory return to A (3:35) that was probably necessitated by Tatum coming suddenly to the end of his available recording time.

Where Tatum's touch is silky smooth, Bud Powell, in his 1951 recording, punches and jabs at the keyboard in the bebop style of which he was an undisputed master (figure 5.1). (Listen to example 5.4 ▶.) Paying homage to Tatum, Powell introduces "Over the Rainbow" by running up the keyboard with a dissonant dominant-oriented scale pervaded by whole tones, his signature sonority. Powell plays two choruses of "Over the Rainbow" in the original key of E flat, seeming to draw on Tatum's plan, in which the first chorus (0:05) is fast and in a more "modern" style, while the

FIGURE 5.1 Cover of Bud Powell, *The Amazing Bud Powell* (1952), with "Over the Rainbow." Courtesy of Blue Note Records

second (1:15) is in a more relaxed stride idiom. But Powell returns to the first style for the last B section (2:11) and the return to A, thus giving the song a rounded shape.

In between the phrases of the tune Powell drops in Tatum-esque runs and arpeggios, now based more on whole tones. But at such moments he also creates short and highly profiled melodic gestures that, as has often been pointed out, transfer the techniques of bebop wind players to the right hand of the piano. Characteristic of his playing is the fanfare-like figure Powell inserts after the first A (0:38), which then recurs with modifications after the first (1:13) and second (2:45) reprises of A.

In addition to pervasive whole-tone sonorities, Powell makes many harmonic substitutions for Arlen's original chords. One of the most characteristic, frequently heard in bebop music, is the so-called tritone substitution, involving a dominant harmony whose root lies a tritone away from the expected dominant. On the "-bow" of the first "rainbow" (0:08), Powell replaces Arlen's E♭^{7} with a richly dissonant A^{11} chord, which resolves down by a half step to the original goal, the subdominant chord, A♭. Powell's progression is especially marked because the A^{11} chord is itself preceded by another substitute: instead of Arlen's G-minor chord ("rain-"), Powell prepares the A^{11} with its own dominant, E^7.

Erroll Garner is a virtuoso in the Tatum tradition, sprinkling the music with rapid, flawless runs and arpeggios. He is a master of both block chordal and stride styles. But Garner's "Over the Rainbow," from 1955, is unlike any other. (Listen to example 5.5 ▶.) Clocking in at just over ten and a half minutes and ranging through a wide variety of keyboard idioms, this is really a fantasy on Arlen's song, or perhaps a monumental set of variations.[7] Garner begins in the key of D flat, modulates up a half step to D at the penultimate full A section (8:07), then for the final A (9:20) moves up a further half step to E flat, where he remains. He thus brings us harmonically "over the rainbow" to Arlen's original tonality of E-flat major.

Garner's long introduction, lasting over a minute and a half, seems free, not obviously related to the melody or harmonies of "Over the Rainbow." Over the next nine minutes, he blurs any sense of the song's AABA structure—hence the impression of fantasy or variation—by frequently alternating a single A section with the B. But Garner creates a powerful trajectory for his "Over the Rainbow" that overrides the episodic nature of the performance and the multiplicity of styles. Starting with the third B section (4:25), he builds a group of sections (through the fifth A) that is almost entirely stride-based. Then, at 5:28, he breaks the pattern of alternation to provide three successive A segments that articulate the midpoint of the performance. Finally, at 8:07, with the ninth articulation of the A section, and simultaneously with the modulation to D major, Garner builds to a massive climax, with octaves thundering in contrary motion. After rising another half step to E flat for the final full A, Garner concludes with a coda based on B, but with motivic elements of A mixed in.

Another distinctive aspect of Garner's "Over the Rainbow" is his alteration of Arlen's melody. The very first time through the A section (beginning at 1:39), and each time thereafter, Garner flattens the seventh on the "rain-" of "rainbow" (example 5.3), thus pushing the music toward the subdominant region sooner than in Arlen's original. Garner's flatted seventh, a classic "blue" note, is more than a local melodic-harmonic effect. He may have been inspired in part by the blue skies and bluebirds, which are, however, hopeful images in Harburg's lyrics. The blue mood created by Garner's surprise move is different, darker, and it goes on to color the rest of his "Over the Rainbow," transforming Dorothy's poignant sadness into a more plaintive lament.

EXAMPLE 5.3 Erroll Garner (1955), modification of opening melody

DICK MARX, ANDRÉ PREVIN, AND KEITH JARRETT

If Tatum, Powell, and Garner travel over the rainbow on the fast track, Marx, Previn, and Jarrett take more reflective, poetic journeys. Marx is not as well known as many of the other the pianists who have recorded "Over the Rainbow," but he is no less imaginative. Indeed, his 1955 version is extraordinary in its range of harmonic and metrical shifts and in the sophistication of the overall design. (Listen to example 5.6 ▶.) Marx plays three full choruses of "Over the Rainbow," then a coda consisting of the B section followed by a return to A. The first chorus unfolds in Arlen's original tonic E flat and in ¢ meter. At the end of the A reprise, Marx pauses on a dominant B♭^{7} (1:36), then drops right into D major, a half-step below the original key, for the second chorus. At this point he changes not only the key but also the meter, reinventing Arlen's tune as a flowing waltz in $\frac{6}{8}$ time. The third chorus (2:26) begins in $\frac{6}{8}$ but further modulates to A major. Here the first two A segments, which adhere to their original length (eight measures each), unfold in a free melodic and harmonic style, not directly related to Arlen's original. It is as though the waltz has gotten carried away with itself and "forgotten" the tune.

The B section of Marx's third chorus (2:50) returns to Arlen's melody and basic harmonic structure but remains initially in $\frac{6}{8}$. Then in a remarkable moment he shifts back from $\frac{6}{8}$ to the original ¢ (example 5.4): three eighth notes of $\frac{6}{8}$ magically become four eighth notes in ¢. Marx signals the shift with a short grace-note figure. A few seconds later (at 2:54) he makes a harmonic move from A major to C major. We thus have a double modulation, metrical and harmonic.

EXAMPLE 5.4 Dick Marx (1955), return to original meter in B section

Now comes the A reprise of the third chorus, in C major and in ¢ meter. But we are not yet home. As he did at the end of the very first A reprise (at 1:36), Marx pauses on the dominant seventh (here G^7) and then eases into a coda by playing a mysterious, harmonically ambiguous version of B with parallel diminished sonorities in the right hand (at 3:21). For the final part of this B (3:37), Marx returns to a more conventional melodic and harmonic style and brings the music around to the original dominant, a $B\flat^7$ chord (3:43). Now comes a final A segment in the home key of E-flat major. It could be argued that Marx is even more inventive than Garner in translating Arlen and Harburg's rainbow into purely instrumental terms. Where Garner went for the blues, Marx paints with a palette spanning numerous keys and different meters.

For all his wandering, Marx ends his "Over the Rainbow" back home in the tonic key. Previn follows the rainbow to a new place. (Listen to example 5.7 ▶.) Previn plays two full choruses of the song; they remain in D major until the last A segment (at 3:32), where he modulates to, and then concludes the song in, F major. When we travel over the rainbow, Previn implies with this large-scale change of key, we do not end up exactly where we began. His leisurely tempo for "Over the Rainbow" opens up a vast musical space that he fills, and even stretches, with haunting harmonic and melodic ideas. He develops the motivic and thematic dimensions of Arlen's song, expanding, for example, the second phrase of the first A section by several measures, separating and repeating the short motives for "There's a" (an ascending minor sixth) and "land of" (a major third).

The opening measures of Previn's version are among the most adventurous of any pianist's (example 5.5). He recasts Arlen's I–vi^{7}–iii progression as a cadential one, ii^{7}–V^{7}–iii, with many added chord tones. The first two measures thus set up a parallel to the cadential motion of the second two, which move toward IV. Previn further enriches the first phrase by filling the space between the chords with a motive based on the oscillating minor thirds of song's B theme ("Someday I'll wish upon a star"). These figures sound extraterrestrial, lying well beyond the rainbow: the C♯ and A♯ eighth notes are not part of the opening half-diminished chord.

EXAMPLE 5.5 André Previn (1960), opening measures, with harmonic analysis

"Over the Rainbow" is one of the first numbers to which Keith Jarrett turned when he began doing more classic jazz improvisation on standard tunes in the later 1970s. He has played it many times in concert, often as an encore. Both Previn and Jarrett take broad tempi for "Over the Rainbow," with a quarter note in the range of the mid- to low 50s. This is slower than many other pianists and significantly below Garland's original (♩ = 88). But even more than for Previn, "Over the Rainbow" becomes for Jarrett a venue for quiet introspection, an interior rainbow (figure 5.2).

Five different Jarrett versions of "Over the Rainbow" exist on recording or video. The longest of these, also containing the greatest amount of free improvisation, is a London performance of 1991 that lasts just over seven minutes. But even the shorter versions that hew more closely to the structure of Arlen's original are expansive. There are many consistencies among Jarrett's recordings of "Over the Rainbow." He always plays the song in F major. Although not straying far from Arlen's original harmonies, Jarrett enhances them by adding tones and unusual voicings, and he animates the texture with inner parts and rich counterpoint. The melody,

FIGURE 5.2 Keith Jarrett at Symphony Hall, Boston (2000). Photo: Patrick Hinely, Work/Play®

always identifiable, is refracted through a variety of rhythmic figures, which are often suspended across beats or bar lines. All these features give Jarrett's playing a unique blend of fluidity and hesitation.

Though not as epic as Garner's, Jarrett's renowned 1995 La Scala version of "Over the Rainbow" similarly diffuses the song's structure in a broad rondo-like design: A–A–B–A–B–A–B(free)–A–coda.[8] (Listen to example 5.8 ▶.) At the third statement of the A section (at 1:39), Jarrett makes an elegant modification in the vein of Previn. Instead of resolving to the tonic, the bass of the dominant chord played at the end of the B section begins a stepwise descending line—C–B–B♭–A—that leads to the iii chord on the second measure.

Jarrett's final B section (at 3:26; example 5.6) provides a beautiful example of his skill at improvising countermelodies. Above Arlen's oscillating eighth notes Jarrett places a thematic idea, already suggested in an earlier run through the B section, which now blossoms into a full, independent tune. Jarrett manages to convey the tenderness of Arlen's elementary piano exercise with a sophisticated transparency that rivals moments in that other great musical portrait of a child's imagination, Robert Schumann's *Scenes from Childhood.*

EXAMPLE 5.6 Keith Jarrett (1995), final B section

All of the pianists discussed in this chapter create something new but instantly recognizable from Arlen's rich harmonic and melodic language. They do so in ways that, even in the absence of Harburg's lyrics, capture important aspects of the meanings of "Over the Rainbow." In the next chapter we will examine another immensely popular version of the song that has carried it into cultural spaces far removed from Kansas, Oz, Judy Garland, and the world of jazz.

CHAPTER 6

THE ISLAND RAINBOW

At 3:00 A.M. one day in 1988, so the story goes, a recording engineer working late in his Honolulu studio received a call from a manager whose client, a singer named Israel Kamakawiwo'ole, wanted to come in right away to record a demo. The engineer was not familiar with Kamakawiwo'ole, then a member of a popular Hawaiian group called the Makaha Sons of Ni'ihau. He reluctantly agreed to make the tape. The recording session was casual, completed in less than twenty minutes. In a high tenor voice, accompanying himself on the ukulele, Kamakawiwo'ole sang—and perhaps largely improvised—a medley of "Over the Rainbow" and "What a Wonderful

World," a song composed by Bob Thiele and George David Weiss and made popular by Louis Armstrong.[1] The medley moves seamlessly over five minutes from "Rainbow" (about two and a half minutes) to "World" (one and a half), and then back to "Rainbow." (Listen to example 6.1 ▶.)

Whether or not this middle-of-the-night session occurred exactly as has been reported, "Rainbow"/"World" would become by far the most familiar version of the Arlen-Harburg ballad and the biggest selling recording by the Hawaiian artist known as "Bruddah Iz" or simply "IZ" (a nickname we will use here). The 1988 medley would achieve its greatest renown when released on IZ's 1993 album *Facing Future*, the first by any Hawaiian artist or group to be certified platinum by the Recording Industry Association of America, with sales of over one million.

IZ died in 1997 at the age of thirty-eight of complications from morbid obesity; he reportedly weighed over a thousand pounds at his death. But his legend has lived on and only grown. The single track of "Rainbow"/"World" has by now sold millions of digital copies. As of this writing, it has spent a record-breaking 380 weeks at or near the top of the *Billboard* World Digital Songs chart.[2] "Rainbow"/"World" (often just the "Rainbow" portion) has also appeared in numerous commercials, in television series, and in films, as we will see below.

So ubiquitous is it, and so complete is the association between the song and the artist, that today many (perhaps most) people around the world believe that IZ composed the song himself. He did not, of course, though arguably more than anyone who has recorded the song since Garland, IZ has given it a new identity. IZ's "Rainbow" is at once strongly tied to time and place in late twentieth-century Hawaii and also global, maybe timeless, in its appeal.

THE RAINBOW AND HAWAIIAN SELF-DETERMINATION

In the cover photo of *Facing Future* we see IZ from behind, clad in a patterned Hawaiian sarong, his long hair flowing loose (figure 6.1). He stands beside a pahu, a traditional drum, looking out over a lush green landscape toward the

FIGURE 6.1 Cover of IZ's album *Facing Future* (1993)

Pacific Ocean, over which arches a large rainbow. The rainbow is no mere decorative touch in this image. A frequent natural occurrence in the Hawaiian archipelago, it has long been an important symbol in native Hawaiian culture. Several islands have prehistoric stone carvings of the so-called Rainbow Man and Rainbow Woman, in which the human figures appear to have a rainbow extending above their heads. A rainbow adorns the state's license plate, and drawings or photographs of rainbows appear on many tourist brochures and websites. A popular destination on the island of Hawaii (the Big Island) is Rainbow Falls, where on sunny mornings rainbows arise from the mist thrown up by the waterfall. The athletic teams of the University of Hawaii have long been known as the Rainbow Warriors, whose uniforms feature rainbow stripes. (In 2000 the university dropped "rainbow" from the teams' nickname, because of what they saw as an implied connection to the LGBT movement. In 2013, the original name was reinstated, apparently because university and team officials regretted the earlier action.)

The cover of *Facing Future* is reminiscent of the classic "Rückenfigur" (a German term meaning a figure seen from the back) that has long been popular in European art, as in some well-known paintings by the nineteenth-century painter Caspar David Friedrich. In such works, we as viewers take in both the individual human subject and the vast natural scene he or she is contemplating. The human figure is at once central and diminished in significance. The cover of *Facing Future*, a modern variation on this theme, does not simply celebrate IZ and his native landscape. For Hawaiians, if less so for the mainlanders and the global community who helped propel this album to the top of the charts, the imagery and musical content of *Facing Future* evoke directly the politics of Hawaiian sovereignty. The association is made clear by the inscription written by IZ that appears on the inside cover in all upper-case letters:

> FACING BACKWARDS I SEE THE PAST
> OUR NATION GAINED, OUR NATION LOST
> OUR SOVEREIGNTY GONE
> OUR LANDS GONE
> ALL TRADED FOR THE PROMISE OF PROGRESS
> WHAT WOULD THEY SAY . . .
> WHAT CAN WE SAY?

Self-determination has been an important issue for Hawaiians ever since their islands were annexed by the United States, first as a territory in 1898, then as a state in 1959. Although statehood was approved by 93 percent of voters, subsequent decades saw the growth of various movements focused on the rights of Native Hawaiians. Some argued for an independent Hawaiian nation, others for a federally recognized status similar to the tribal sovereignty granted to Native Americans.

Along with this political advocacy came promotion of indigenous Hawaiian culture. In the so-called Hawaiian Renaissance, arising in the 1970s, native musicians hybridized Hawaiian music with other popular styles from around the world. Many songs had lyrics of dissent or protest.[3] IZ was a part of this phenomenon early on. The Makaha Sons of Ni'ihau, which he and his brother Skippy helped found in 1975, sang songs in both English and Hawaiian, some with explicitly political themes, addressing, for example, the American military maneuvers that had destroyed sacred sites during World War II.

After he left the Makaha Sons and formed his own band, IZ continued to perform and record Hawaiian songs on themes of protest. *Facing Future* was the brainchild of IZ's manager and producer, Jon de Mello of Mountain Apple Company. The critic Dan Kois has described the album as "a cannily constructed mélange of traditional Hawaiian folk singing, 'Jawaiian' island reggae, and movie-trailer-ready bombast."[4] In these ways, *Facing Future* is a prime example of hybridity in world music, which involves the mixing of widely different traditions.[5]

Facing Future is framed by two slightly different versions of the same number, "Hawai'i '78," a song of protest written in 1978 by Mickey Ioane in connection with the arrest of Hawaiian demonstrators in a confrontation with the Army National Guard over land-rights issues. The Makaha Sons recorded "Hawai'i '78" the following year, and it became their biggest hit. The song includes a mixture of Hawaiian and English lyrics, including a kind of refrain, "Cry for the gods, cry for the people / Cry for the land that was taken away / And then yet you'll find Hawai'i." In the first, introductory version of "Hawai'i '78" on *Facing Future*, sung segments are interspersed with voiceovers of IZ reminiscing about his father and his early life.

The remaining thirteen tracks of *Facing Future* are divided between Hawaiian and English-language numbers. The nine Hawaiian songs celebrate or memorialize various aspects of indigenous life, including family, romantic love, food, streetcars, landscape, and a devastating tsunami. The three songs in English, in addition to "Rainbow"/"World," are the love song "White Sandy Beach of Hawai'i," recorded in the same late-night session in 1988; a version of John Denver's 1971 song "Take Me Home, Country Roads"; and "Maui Hawaiian Sup'pa Man," about a legendary "superman" figure. Kois calls the latter two songs "the ne plus ultra of the Jawaiian sound," a reggae-influenced style that has been popular since the 1980s. These two songs were initially the most successful radio hits from the album, before "Rainbow"/"World" took off.

IZ was ambivalent about including the track on *Facing Future*. But de Mello felt strongly about how well rainbows, Hawaii, and the medley worked together. As the critic Nate Chinen notes, "Kamakawiwo'ole was someone who had actually resided in a land of rainbows. With his version he managed to make the song both sweeter and sadder, using it not to express longing for a paradise unseen but for a paradise lost, or more precisely, occupied and annexed: an Oz becoming Kansas, right before his eyes."[6] IZ was persuaded, and, according to Kois, the medley "was sneaked in near the end of the record," as the penultimate track before the recapitulation of "Hawai'i '78." De Mello ultimately came to regret the placement: "If I thought it was gonna be the top dog, do you think I'd put that in as track number fourteen?"[7]

The medley fits perfectly with the larger message of *Facing Future*. "Rainbow" longs for a paradise not yet reached, not yet at hand. "World" suggests that such a place exists and is not yet lost. This understanding of "World" was articulated directly by Louis Armstrong in a recording of 1970, made at the height of the Vietnam War and the era of student protests. In a spoken voiceover at the beginning, Armstrong gave the song a political spin. He said, "Some of you young folks been saying to me: 'Hey, Pops, what do you mean, what a wonderful world? How about all them wars all over the place. You call them wonderful? And how about hunger and pollution? They ain't so wonderful either.' But how about listening to old Pops for a minute? Seems to me it ain't the world that's so bad but what we're doin' to it. And all I'm saying is: see what a wonderful world it would be if only we'd give it a chance."[8]

The irony acknowledged in Armstrong's comments—how can you sing about a "wonderful" world today?—was made explicit for a new generation when the song was used in the soundtrack of the 1987 film *Good Morning, Vietnam.* The Armed Forces Radio DJ, played by Robin Williams, puts Armstrong's "World" on the air after his usual effusive (and ironic) morning greeting. As it plays, we see scenes from the lives of military men and Vietnamese people, including images of devastation, violence, and death.

"RAINBOW" AND "WORLD" GET "ISRAELIZED"

On the list of tracks for *Facing Future* the title of the John Denver song, "Take Me Home, Country Roads," appears as "Take Me Home Country Road," in the singular, with no comma. IZ freely recasts the lyrics, substituting Hawaiian images for North American ones: "West Virginia" becomes "West Makaha," "Shenandoah River" becomes "crystal clear blue water," and so forth. IZ's "Take Me Home Country Road" is an example of what some Hawaiian commentators have called, with either disdain or admiration, a song being "Israelized."[9]

"Rainbow" and "World" are likewise Israelized in the medley, in ways that enhance connections between the two. Their original lyrics already share imagery that clearly appealed to IZ. The rainbow of the first song is echoed in the "colors of the rainbow" identified in the second: "trees of green," "red roses," "skies of blue," and "clouds of white." But "World" also humanizes or domesticates the rainbow, since the colors, "so pretty in the sky," are "also on the faces of people passing by." IZ makes the first transition between the songs by moving directly from the "I" of "why can't I?" that ends "Rainbow" into the "I" of "I see trees of green," the first line of "World."

Even in their original forms "Rainbow" and "World" share certain melodic and harmonic features. On the phrase "way up high" in "Rainbow" the tune rises from the tonic to the sixth degree of the scale and then falls to the fifth, a pattern very similar to "*trees* of green, *red roses too*" in "World" (at the words indicated in italics). IZ harmonizes the opening measures of both songs, which he performs in C major, with the same progression, I–V–IV–I, a modification of the chords they share in their original form. IZ makes other harmonic associations between the songs, especially in his use of the vi chord (A minor). He begins "Rainbow" with a four-bar ukulele riff on the progression I–V–vi–I. Then comes an eight-bar introductory wordless vocalise on "Ooh," where vi becomes the harmonic goal, strengthened by a cadence from its own dominant seventh chord (E^7). This same E^7–A-minor cadence appears in "World," both in the original and in IZ's versions, at the words "I'll watch them bloom *for me and you.*"

The Israelization of "Over the Rainbow" likewise involves many changes in the melody and words. At the beginning of the song, IZ sings:

Somewhere over the rainbow,
Way up high,
And the dreams that you dream of,
Once in a lullaby.

Singing these lines, IZ avoids Arlen's opening octave leap, beginning with repeated pitches on "Somewhere." In the third line, he sings the original notes with words adapted from later in the chorus, instead of Harburg's "There's a land that I heard of." Then in the fourth line he sings the original words to a new melody. IZ makes similar alterations throughout the song. Although Kois suggests that IZ "screws up" in making these changes, they are fully consistent with the ethos of Israelization, probably a result of late-night spontaneity, not misremembering.

To be Israelized is in an important sense to be Hawaiianized. IZ's "Rainbow" contains a number of signifiers of Hawaiian music, first and foremost, of course, the ukulele. In a spoken introductory segment almost always cut when the track is played, IZ dedicates the song, in the Hawaiian language, to his idol, the iconic Hawaiian musician Gabby Pahinui. In the bridge section IZ follows Harburg's lyrics but invents a new melody that reimagines Arlen's oscillation between pitches (the imitation of the child's piano exercise) in the style of a chant, often called *kahiko*, used to accompany hula dancing.[10] Example 6.1 juxtaposes IZ's bridge melody with a traditional hula chant; both alternate initially between two pitches a fourth apart (C–G).

EXAMPLE 6.1 (a) IZ's melody for the B section of "Over the Rainbow"; (b) tune of "Ipo Lei Manu / Hula Kui," from Amy Ku'uleailoha Stillman, "Textualizing Hawaiian Music," *American Music* 23 (2005): 87

IZ'S "RAINBOW" ON TELEVISION AND FILM

Over the past twenty-five years IZ's "Rainbow" has transcended its Hawaiian roots in ways that he and his producers could scarcely have imagined at the beginning, but which have since brought enormous revenue to de Mello's Mountain Apple Company. Fans can purchase, for example, a "Musical Message in a Bottle," intended for those "looking for a special way to send some aloha to someone"; the song plays when the lid is lifted.[11] IZ's "Over the Rainbow" has been widely licensed for television commercials, where it is used (sometimes with "World," sometimes without) to promote the Norwegian lottery, Dutch health insurance, Austrian sugar, Korean cosmetics, American and Hungarian banks, AT&T cellular services, Rice Krispies, Fiat Croma cars (endorsed by Jeremy Irons), Lynx body spray, and eToys.[12] (View example 6.2 ▶.) Although the contexts and intended markets differ widely among these commercials, none references the Hawaiianness of IZ's "Over the Rainbow." Instead, the song provides an optimistic, feel-good, and occasionally tongue-in-cheek sonic backdrop for the sales pitch.

IZ's "Rainbow" also occurs at the end of the final episode of the first season of *Glee* (June 8, 2010). (View example 6.3 ▶.) After the singing group New Directions, coached by glee club director Will Schuester (Matthew Morrison), loses the regional competition, its members are supposed to give up their rehearsal space at the high school. But the intervention of Schuester's nemesis Sue Sylvester (Jane Lynch) gets the group a year's reprieve. In the last scene, after announcing the good news, Schuester (playing ukulele) and one of the students, Puck (playing guitar), serenade the group with their own cover of IZ's "Rainbow" (figure 6.2). During the song, we cut briefly to see the character of Shelby (Idina Menzel) adopting the baby of Puck and another student, Quinn. IZ's "Rainbow" is thus associated again with loss and sadness (the failure of New Direction), but also with optimism (the group's reprieve and the adoption of the baby).

IZ's "Rainbow" projects a more complex set of meanings in other film and television soundtracks. Often, and perhaps surprisingly, the song is associated with death, but also with rebirth or hope. *Meet Joe Black* (1998) and *Finding Forrester* (2000) are both movies with bittersweet endings involving the loss of an older male character (played by Anthony Hopkins and Sean Connery, respectively), but also promising a bright future for younger people they have loved or mentored (the couple Claire Forlani and Brad

FIGURE 6.2 Will (Matthew Morrison) sings and plays ukulele in a cover of IZ's "Over the Rainbow" on *Glee* (2010)

Pitt, the high school student Rob Brown). In both films, IZ's song appears at the very end, clearly intended to convey something of this muted optimism. In *Meet Joe Black* it is heard over the credits as a foil to the film's symphonic soundtrack by Thomas Newman, which includes a fully scored segment from "World" in the final scene. In *Finding Forrester* IZ is heard in the last minutes (and then over the credits) as the camera pans around the apartment of the now-dead writer William Forrester and before moving to the street below, where his teenage mentee Jamal plays basketball with a friend.

Perhaps the most powerfully affecting appearance of IZ's "Rainbow," because it fits both the geographic and narrative dimensions of the plot, occurs at the death of the main character Dr. Mark Greene in the long-running television series *ER* (season 8, episode 21, broadcast May 9, 2002). (View example 6.4 ▶.) Greene, suffering from an inoperable brain tumor, moves from Chicago to Hawaii, where he had spent happy times in his childhood. As he lies dying on his bed, we hear the ocean waves in the background. His formerly estranged teenage daughter Rachel tells him how she remembers a lullaby that Greene used to sing her. She puts a pair of headphones over his ears. As he smiles and closes his eyes for the last time, IZ's version of "Rainbow" replaces the ocean on the soundtrack. As the song continues for about two minutes, a series of flashbacks alternates with images of Greene lying on his deathbed: Rachel, his current wife Elizabeth and their small baby, and the Chicago hospital where Greene worked. The song fades from the soundtrack when Elizabeth comes in the next day to find him dead.

The *ER* scene poignantly captures two elements of IZ's "Rainbow." First, Rachel's explicit identification of the song as a lullaby reflects the "once in a lullaby" of Harburg's lyrics. The song Greene sang to put Rachel to sleep as a child is now given back to him to ease him into death. Second, the flashbacks feature the ocean, the beach, and the trees of the Hawaiian landscape. As in the films discussed above, IZ's "Rainbow" carries a double-edged affect in the *ER* segment: sadness and poignancy at Greene's death, but also reassurance that life carries on.

IZ died in Hawaii in July 1997, five years before the fictional Mark Greene. Two days after the funeral, his ashes were scattered into the Pacific Ocean at Makua Beach on

Oahu. Thousands gathered on the shore and in kayaks, on sailboats, and floating on surfboards. Scenes from the event are included on the official music video of "Over the Rainbow" released by Mountain Apple, which has been viewed almost 300 million times. (View example 6.5 ▶.) "IZ Lives," reads the prophetic inscription visible on one of the sails.

EPILOGUE

IZ's "OVER THE RAINBOW" projects a utopian vision of Hawaii as a land of natural beauty and indigenous pride. Although threatened, IZ's home is nonetheless a paradise, already over (and under) the rainbow. In its original context in *The Wizard of Oz*, as we have seen, "Over the Rainbow" had a less stable message. The creation of the film was marked by ambiguity—even confusion—about Dorothy's Kansas song: would it celebrate the values of home, even when home is unwelcoming, or the desire to seek out an unknown but happier place? Harburg, who objected to the home-sweet-home "tripe," created with Arlen a ballad that has been almost universally recognized as a plea to escape. Yet there is no question that *The Wizard of Oz* celebrates, musically and dramatically, the theme of home sweet home.

Commentators have sought to unpack the apparent contradictions. In 1984 the philosopher of religion Linda

Hansen argued that although Dorothy needs to leave Kansas, hers is ultimately a search to feel "at home" wherever she is in the world. As Hansen recognizes, Dorothy's story is an archetypal quest narrative, or perhaps a version of a Bildungsroman, in which a character embarks on a journey through which he or she will gain wisdom and experience. "Home is not a place 'out there' to be found," Hansen suggests, "but a power—like intelligence, love, or courage—to be developed." When Dorothy does return home to Kansas at the end of the film, she has changed and matured. "*This* world is not now Kansas as Auntie Em and Uncle Henry see it, but Kansas as Dorothy sees it. Oz is not a separate world from Kansas, but her vision of what is possible *in* Kansas."[1]

Hansen sees Dorothy's transformation as a religious one, arguing that Oz represents "Dorothy's grace, her chance to participate in the sacred work of making our world a home" (101). Few viewers of the film might follow her that far. But in a monograph of 1992, Salman Rushdie sacralizes "Over the Rainbow" as a "hymn to Elsewhere":

> Anybody who has swallowed the scriptwriters' notion that this is a film about the superiority of "home" over "away," that the moral of *The Wizard of Oz* is as sickly-sweet as an embroidered sampler—"East, West, home's best"—would do well to listen to the yearning in Judy Garland's voice, as her face tilts up towards the skies. What she expresses here, what she embodies with the purity of an archetype, is the human dream of *leaving*, a dream at least as powerful as its countervailing dream of roots. . . . "Over the Rainbow" is, or ought to be, the anthem of all the world's migrants, all those who go in search of the place where "the dreams that you dare to dream really do come true."

> It is a celebration of Escape, a grand paean to the uprooted self, a hymn—*the* hymn—to Elsewhere.[2]

Rushdie's characterization of "Over the Rainbow" as a hymn resonates with my suggestion in chapter 3 that some aspects of the song, including the plagal cadences in the first phrases, can be heard as markers of sacred music. But his reading of "Over the Rainbow" as "a hymn to Elsewhere" is more political than religious. Although Rushdie had known and loved *The Wizard of Oz* since childhood, the idea of an "uprooted self" had special resonance for him in the early 1990s. After the publication of his novel *The Satanic Verses*, the Iranian supreme leader Ayatollah Khomeini issued a fatwa saying Muslims had a duty to kill Rushdie, who then had to live under police protection for nine years in England.

Like Hansen, Rushdie sees "home" more as a concept than a specific place. "The real secret of the ruby slippers is not that 'there's no place like home,'" he argues, "but rather that there is no longer any such place *as* home: except, of course, for the home we make, or the homes that are made for us, in Oz, which is anywhere and everywhere, except the place from which we began" (58).

As Hansen and Rushdie suggest in different ways, *The Wizard of Oz* is ultimately about finding empowerment and acceptance, about realizing one's capacity to create a home and feel at home. "Over the Rainbow" introduces the idea of empowerment into the film when Dorothy sings "Why, oh, why can't I?" The song is not only about wishing ("Someday I'll wish upon a star") but also about achievement ("That's where you'll find me"). By the end of *The Wizard of Oz*, Dorothy has learned that, yes, she *can*.

Harburg reinforced this theme in his work on the film. He wrote the part of the screenplay that takes place in the Throne Room, where the newly humbugged wizard tells Dorothy's companions, who have come to get their heart, brain, and courage, that they have always had these attributes, which are interior and innate. Soon thereafter, Glinda tells Dorothy that she has always had the "power" to return to Kansas simply by wishing herself there. "Then why didn't you tell her before?" the Scarecrow asks Glinda. "Because she wouldn't have believed me," Glinda replies, suggesting that Dorothy had to "learn it for herself" on her quest.

The afterlife of "Over the Rainbow" confirms that the song has come to signify more than mere escape to utopia. Garland kept singing it throughout her career. It became her "theme song" not because she wanted to opt out of life's difficulties but because she fought to continue on. During the early days of gay liberation "Over the Rainbow" spoke to a segment of society that felt marginalized, that wanted inclusion. For IZ, the song (at least when placed on the album *Facing Future*) captured the spirit of Hawaiian self-determination, a desire to preserve a place and a culture that were being threatened by external forces.

"Over the Rainbow" has conveyed similar sentiments in some unexpected contexts. When the singer-songwriter Ingrid Michaelson assembled a group of children from Newtown, Connecticut, to sing "Over the Rainbow" in January 2013, just weeks after the killings at Sandy Hook Elementary School, the message was one not of evasion but of rootedness, of determination that they would not allow their community to be disrupted by the act of a crazed shooter.[3]

In a similar gesture of reassurance and solidarity, on June 4, 2017, the pop star Ariana Grande sang "Over the Rainbow" as the encore at her One Love Manchester concert in England. A benefit for victims of the recent suicide bombing at that city's arena, the event was attended by 50,000, and broadcast and live-streamed to millions more worldwide. Members of the mostly young audience wept during the number, and Grande herself almost broke down in the coda.[4]

In a very different historical and moral context, a gunman whistled "Over the Rainbow" while firing upon his targets. In January 1941 the *New York Times* carried a first-hand account by a British Royal Air Force pilot of a bombing raid on German barges:

> Away ahead there the fireworks have begun—we are whistling down at them at more than four miles a minute—the bomber aimer is now prone on the floor, whistling through his teeth "Over the Rainbow." The whole sky seems to light up with white skeleton figures of searchlights.[5]

We cannot, of course, know what brought this song to the gunner's mind as he took aim at his targets. It may just have been the first tune that came to him. But perhaps "Over the Rainbow" also captured, at least unconsciously, his hopes for a better, safer world at a precarious moment before the Soviet Union and the United States entered the war, when the member states of the British Commonwealth were alone in fighting Germany and the Axis powers.

This episode took place just a year after James Stewart's drunken crooning of the song in the film *The Philadelphia Story*. The contrast between light social comedy and grim wartime reality could not be more extreme. But it also confirms the enormous resonance "Over the Rainbow" has had in different historical, social, political, and cultural contexts since Garland's Dorothy sang it on a gray Kansas farm almost eighty years ago in *The Wizard of Oz*. Over the decades the song has retained its strong association with that singer, that character, and that film, and then more recently with the voice and career of IZ. But we should never forget to give credit to the men behind the curtain, Harold Arlen and Yip Harburg, the real-life wizards that created "Over the Rainbow" and sent it on its way.

ADDITIONAL SOURCES FOR READING AND LISTENING

STANDARD SOURCES ON THE creation of the MGM film *The Wizard of Oz* include Aljean Harmetz, *The Making of the Wizard of Oz* (New York: Limelight, 1984 [orig. 1977]); John Fricke, Jay Scarfone, and William Stillman, *The Wizard of Oz: The Official 50th Anniversary Pictorial History* (New York: Warner, 1989); and Hugh Fordin, *The World of Entertainment! Hollywood's Greatest Musicals* (Garden City, NY: Doubleday, 1975). There are also many features, including commentary, outtakes, and deleted scenes, on the seventy-fifth-anniversary rerelease of *The Wizard of Oz* (Time Warner Video, 2014).

For the screenplay, with background information and the text for some scenes that were cut, see Noel Langley, Florence Ryerson, and Edgar Allan Woolf, *The Wizard of Oz: The Screenplay*, ed. Michael Patrick Hearn (New York: Delta, 1989). The film's entire original soundtrack, along with many outtakes, is included on *The Wizard of Oz: The Deluxe Edition* (Rhino Records, R2 71964, 1995).

The most thorough biography of Harold Arlen is Edward Jablonski, *Harold Arlen: Rhythm, Rainbows, and Blues* (Boston: Northeastern University Press, 1996). On E. Y. Harburg, see Harriet Hyman Alonso, *Yip Harburg: Legendary Lyricist and Human Rights Activist* (Middletown, CT: Wesleyan University Press, 2012). The best critical study of the American popular song repertory, including extensive commentary on Arlen, remains Alec Wilder, *American Popular Song: The Great Innovators, 1900–1950* (New York: Oxford University Press, 1990 [orig. 1972]). See also Allen Forte, *The American Popular Ballad of the Golden Era, 1924–1950* (Princeton, NJ: Princeton University Press, 1995), which includes a chapter on "Over the Rainbow"; and William Zinsser, *Easy to Remember: The Great American Songwriters and Their Songs* (Boston, MA: David R. Godine, 2000).

Garland has been the subject of numerous biographies. Among the most respected is Gerold Frank, *Judy* (New York: Harper & Row, 1975). See also Scott Schechter, *Judy Garland: The Day-by-Day Chronicle of a Legend* (New York: Cooper Square, 2002). The best account of Garland's special relationship with "Over the Rainbow" is John Fricke, "Only One of All Our Millions . . . ," in the *Baum Bugle* 30, no. 2 (Autumn 1986): 3–8. Garland's discography is enormous. A recent CD release, compiled by Garland expert Laurence Schulman, has seven different versions of "Over the Rainbow": *Judy Garland Sings Harold Arlen* (JSP 4246, 2016).

A wonderful survey and demonstration of jazz piano styles is *Dick Hyman's Century of Jazz Piano* (Arbors Records 19348, 2009). Another helpful survey is Robert Doerschuk,

88: The Giants of Jazz Piano (San Francisco: Backbeat, 2001). For detailed consideration of jazz techniques, see Dariusz Terefenko, *Jazz Theory: From Basic to Advanced Study* (New York: Routledge, 2014).

A useful study of the creation and context of Israel Kamakawiwo'ole's recording of "Over the Rainbow" is Dan Kois, *Facing Future* (New York: Continuum, 2010).

NOTES

INTRODUCTION

1 Mel Tormé, *The Other Side of the Rainbow: With Judy Garland on the Dawn Patrol* (New York: Galahad, 1970), 45; Salman Rushdie, *The Wizard of Oz*, 2nd ed. (London: Palgrave Macmillan, 2012), 25.

2 "New Song List Puts 'Rainbow' Way Up High," *CNN Entertainment*, March 7, 2001, http://www.cnn.com/2001/SHOWBIZ/Music/03/07/365.songs/, accessed September 29, 2016; American Film Institute, "AFI's 100 Greatest American Movie Music [*sic*]," http://www.afi.com/100Years/songs.aspx, accessed September 29, 2016.

3 See Todd Decker, *Who Should Sing "Ol' Man River"? The Lives of An American Song* (Oxford: Oxford University Press, 2014); Jeffrey Magee, "Irving Berlin's 'Blue Skies': Ethnic Affiliates and Musical Transformations," *Musical Quarterly* 84 (2000): 537–80; Sheryl Kaskowitz, *God Bless America: The Surprising History of an Iconic Song* (Oxford and New York: Oxford University Press, 2013); and Jody Rosen, *White Christmas: The Story of an American Song* (New York: Scribner, 2002).

4 See https://youtu.be/U9u1V2MUUak and https://youtu.be/QcBYpmD29ik, accessed April 24, 2017.

CHAPTER 1

1 Edward Jablonski, *Harold Arlen: Rhythm, Rainbows, and Blues* (Boston: Northeastern University Press, 1996), 126.

2 L. Frank Baum, *The Wonderful Wizard of Oz* (Chicago: George M. Hill, 1900), 12. Further references are to this edition.

3 Aljean Harmetz, *The Making of "The Wizard of Oz"* (New York: Limelight, 1984 [orig. 1977]), 37.

4 See Henry M. Littlefield, "The Wizard of Oz: Parable on Populism," *American Quarterly* 16 (1964): 47–58, and David B. Parker, "The Rise and Fall of *The*

Wonderful Wizard of Oz as a 'Parable on Populism,'" *Journal of the Georgia Association of Historians* 15 (1994): 49–63.

5 Peter Kaplan, "Yip Harburg Beyond the Rainbow," *Washington Post*, February 28, 1981, B2.

6 See Francis MacDonnell, "'The Emerald City Was the New Deal': E. Y. Harburg and *The Wonderful Wizard of Oz*," *Journal of American Culture* 13 (1990): 71–75.

7 Roger Edens Collection, CAL, Box 12A.

8 Charles Hamm, *Yesterdays: Popular Song in America* (New York: W. W. Norton, 1979), 165.

9 A small sampling would include "If I Only Had a Home Sweet Home" (1906) by A. L. McDermott and J. Johns, "In the Harbor of Home Sweet Home" (1910) by A. J. Holmes and C. M. Dennison, and Irving Berlin's "I Love to Stay at Home" (1915).

10 MHL, Turner/MGM Scripts, W-987, p. 2.

11 Laura Lynn Broadhurst, "Wonderful Wizards of Song: Harold Arlen, E. Y. 'Yip' Harburg, and the Creation of the Songs for MGM's *The Wizard of Oz*" (Ph.D. dissertation in progress, Rutgers University).

12 A facsimile of Edens's handwritten Munchkin sequence outline (CAL Edens Collection) is in John Fricke, Jay Scarfone, and William Stillman, *The Wizard of Oz: The Official 50th Anniversary Pictorial History* (New York: Warner, 1989), 41.

13 LL, Wizard of Oz Mss. Collection (LMC 2090), Box 1, Folder 6.

14 LL, Oz Collection, Box 1, Folder 8.

15 LL, Oz Collection, Box 2, Folder 23.

16 Harmetz, *Making of "The Wizard of Oz,"* 57.

17 See Elisabeth Bronfen, *Home in Hollywood: The Imaginary Geography of Cinema* (New York: Columbia University Press, 2004), and Richard F. Selcer, "Home Sweet Movies: From Tara to Oz and Home Again," *Journal of Popular Film and Television* 18 (1990): 52–63.

18 Memo from Arthur Freed, January 31, 1938, reproduced in Hugh Fordin, *The World of Entertainment! Hollywood's Greatest Musicals* (Garden City, NY: Doubleday, 1975), 14.

19 Fricke, Scarfone, and Stillman, *Wizard of Oz*, 30.

20 Harriet Hyman Alonso, *Yip Harburg: Legendary Lyricist and Human Rights Activist* (Middletown, CT: Wesleyan University Press, 2012), 82–83.

21 Edward Jablonski, *Happy With the Blues* (New York: Da Capo, 1986 [orig. 1961]), 120.

22 Arlen, interview with Walter Cronkite on the CBS television show *The Twentieth Century*, broadcast February 9, 1964. Transcript courtesy of the Yip Harburg Foundation, p. 5.

23 Edward Jablonski, *Harold Arlen: Rhythm, Rainbows, and Blues* (Boston: Northeastern University Press, 1996), 131.

24 Michael Feinstein, *Nice Work If You Can Get It: My Life in Rhythm and Rhyme* (New York: Hyperion, 1995), 285.

25 The conflicting aspects of Arlen's and Harburg's accounts of the genesis of "Over the Rainbow" are summarized in Alonso, *Yip Harburg*, 105–6.

26 IGL, Harburg Collection, Box 2, Folder 14.

27 Harmetz, *Making of "The Wizard of Oz,"* 81.

28 Harold Meyerson and Ernie Harburg, *Who Put the Rainbow in "The Wizard of Oz"?: Yip Harburg, Lyricist* (Ann Arbor: University of Michigan Press, 1993), 134.

29 IGL, Harburg Collection, Box 2, Folder 14.

30 Broadhurst, "Wonderful Wizards of Song."

CHAPTER 2

1 LL, Oz Collection, Box 2, Folder 6.

2 This shooting script forms the basis of Noel Langley, Florence Ryerson, and Edgar Allan Woolf, *The Wizard of Oz: The Screenplay*, ed. Michael Patrick Hearn (New York: Delta, 1989). Hearn, who notes the discrepancy in the lyrics for the bridge of "Over the Rainbow" (39–40), is, however, wrong to suggest that "the final tag [coda] was added at the time of the scene's filming." The coda is clearly present in the piano-vocal score of June 29, 1938.

3 MHL, Turner/MGM Scripts, W-989.

4 *The Wizard of Oz Continuity Script, March 15, 1939* (n.p.: Turner Entertainment and MGM/UA Home Video, 1993), Reel 1, pp. 6–7.

5 The memo is reproduced in John Fricke and Jonathan Shirshekan, *The Wizard of Oz: An Illustrated Companion to the Classic Movie* (New York: Metro, 2009), 34.

6 Broadhurst, "Wonderful Wizards of Song." The screenplay draft is in LL, Oz Collection, Box 1, Folder 10. The page is dated July 1.

7 The recording can be heard on the CD set *The Wizard of Oz: The Deluxe Edition*, Rhino Records R2 71964, (1995), disc 2, track 34.

8 The reprise is still present in the continuity script of March 15, 1939. See *The Wizard of Oz Continuity Script*, Reel 10, p. 2.

9 Langley, Ryerson, and Woolf, *Wizard of Oz*, appendix E. Further references will be to this source.

10 MHL, Turner/MGM Scripts, W-989. These revisions are likely the work of the screenwriter John Lee Mahin, who worked closely with Victor Fleming on the film throughout the late fall and winter of 1938–39. See Hearn's introduction to Langley, Ryerson, and Woolf, *Wizard of Oz*, 23–25.

11 Harmetz, *Making of "The Wizard of Oz,"* 165.
12 Fricke, Scarfone, and Stillman, *Wizard of Oz*, 107.
13 Fordin, *World of Entertainment*, 27
14 Alonso, *Yip Harburg*, 89.
15 Jablonski, *Harold Arlen*, 121.
16 Personal communication with Bea Wain's daughter Bonnie Barnes (email of December 31, 2013), who asked the questions of her mother and then conveyed the answers to me.
17 Fricke, Scarfone, and Stillman, *Wizard of Oz*, 126.
18 Letter from former MGM archives; photocopy provided to the author by John Fricke. All further citations are from this correspondence.
19 Gordon Wright, "Pretty Stuff," *Metronome*, April 1939, 50.
20 Jazz Records released the complete *Good News* broadcast on CD in 1991, *Behind the Scenes at the Making of "The Wizard of Oz,"* J-CD-629.
21 See the detailed account of Garland's activities in Scott Schechter, *Judy Garland: The Day-by-Day Chronicle of a Legend* (New York: Cooper Square, 2002). The year 1939 is chronicled on pp. 51–62.
22 Recording dates are taken from Tom Lord, *The Jazz Discography*, http://www.lordisco.com, accessed December 31, 2016.
23 Joel Whitburn, *Pop Memories, 1890–1954* (Menomonee Falls, WI: Record Research, 1986), 85, 114, 170, 309.

CHAPTER 3

1 Alec Wilder, *American Popular Song: The Great Innovators, 1920–1950* (New York: Oxford University Press, 1990 [orig. 1972]), 290.
2 Jablonski, *Happy with the Blues*, 91.
3 Wilson's score has not been published, but he has performed it with several orchestras, synchronized to the film. See http://www.johnwilsonorchestra.com/about-the-music/john-wilson/, accessed October 2, 2016.
4 Quoted in Harmetz, *Making of "The Wizard of Oz,"* 97.
5 The introduction can be heard on its own, without Dorothy's spoken words, on the Rhino CD set *The Wizard of Oz*, disc 1, track 4.
6 See Nathan Platte, "Nostalgia, the Silent Cinema, and the Art of Quotation in Herbert Stothart's Score for *The Wizard of Oz* (1939)," *Journal of Film Music* 4 (2011): 45–64.
7 I am grateful to Jeff Magee (personal communication) for suggesting the association with "Miss Lucy Long." The proposal of "Round and Round the Village" comes from Platte, "Nostalgia, the Silent Cinema," 48. The excerpts in my example (transposed to the key of A flat) are taken from the Levy Sheet Music Collection at the Milton S. Eisenhower Library at Johns Hopkins

University, https://jscholarship.library.jhu.edu/bitstream/handle/1774.2/13391/017.135b.001.webimage.JPEG?sequence=1, accessed October 4, 2016, for "Miss Lucy Long," and from Alice B. Gomme, ed., *Children's Singing Games*, 2nd ser., ed. (London: David Nutt, 1894), 41, for "Round and Round the Village."

8 *The Wizard of Oz*, disc 2, track 15.

CHAPTER 4

1 Jablonski, *Happy With the Blues*, 121.

2 "Judy Garland, 47, Found Dead," *New York Times*, June 23, 1969, available online at https://www.nytimes.com/books/00/04/09/specials/garland-obit.html, accessed August 31, 2015.

3 John Fricke, "Only One of All Our Millions . . . ," in *Baum Bugle* 30, no. 2 (Autumn 1986): 5. Unless otherwise noted, further quotations from Garland about Dorothy are from this source.

4 The most complete listings of Garland's many performances of "Over the Rainbow," in film, on disc, on radio, and on television, can be found by consulting two valuable websites: the Judy Room, http://www.thejudyroom.com/discography.html#nil, and the Judy Garland Database, http://www.jgdb.com/musndx.htm, both accessed August 7, 2016.

5 Transcribed from an MP3 recording provided by Will Friedwald. See the listing for this recording (which may not have been broadcast) on the Judy Garland Database, accessed October 7, 2016, http://www.jgdb.com/radio44.htm.

6 John C. Skipper, *Meredith Willson: The Unsinkable Music Man* (El Dorado Hills, CA: Savas, 2000), 81. The Judy Room (http://www.thejudyroom.com/misc/dicktracycd.html, accessed October 7, 2016) suggests the recording of *Dick Tracy in B-Flat* was made February 20, not February 15. The recording was released on CD in 1999 by Howard's International (HS 4010).

7 Tormé, *Other Side of the Rainbow*, 45.

8 See Emily R. Coleman, *The Complete Judy Garland* (New York: Harper & Row, 1990), 224. A facsimile of the program is at Charlie Dale's blog *My Journey with Judy*, October 14, 2008, http://myjourneywithjudy.blogspot.com/2008/10/robin-hood-dell-concert-program-1943.html, accessed October 7, 2016.

9 The *Ford Star Jubilee* broadcast is available (though incomplete) on DVD from Synergy Entertainment (2003).

10 *Judy at Carnegie Hall*, 40th anniversary CD reissue, Capitol Records 27876, (2001).

11 This memo is reproduced in facsimile in Fricke, Scarfone, and Stillman, *Wizard of Oz*, 44.

12 This concert was called "A Cavalcade of American Music by Those Who Make America's Music." It is reproduced on CD under the title *Carousel of American Music*, Music & Arts CD 971, (1997).

13 Emily Coleman, liner notes for *Judy Garland: The One and Only,* Capitol Records C2 96600, (1991), pp. 6–7.

14 Steven Frank, "What Does It Take To Be a Gay Icon Today?,"*NewNowNext*, September 2005, 2007, http://www.newnownext.com/what-does-it-take-to-be-a-gay-icon-today/09/2007/3/, accessed November 1, 2015.

15 Personal communication (email of July 16, 2016).

16 An excellent critical survey of these intersections is Dee Michel, *Friends of Dorothy: Why Gay Boys and Gay Men Love* The Wizard of Oz (forthcoming, Northampton, MA: Phil Michaels Publications), especially chapter 9, "Oz and Judy in Gay Folklore."

17 Dee Michel, "Not in Kansas Anymore: The Appeal of Oz for Gay Males," *Baum Bugle* 46, no. 1 (Spring 2002): 34.

18 Michel, "Not in Kansas Anymore," 33.

19 Richard Dyer, "Judy Garland and Gay Men," in *Heavenly Bodies: Film Stars and Society*, 2nd ed. (London: Routledge, 2004), 165. Further references will be given in the text.

20 Michael Joseph Gross, "The Queen is Dead," *Atlantic*, August 2000, http://www.theatlantic.com/magazine/archive/2000/08/the-queen-is-dead/378302/, accessed November 23, 2015.

21 Robert Leleux, "The Road Gets Rougher for Judyism's Faithful," *New York Times*, April 5, 2012, available online at http://www.nytimes.com/2012/04/06/arts/judy-garland-gay-idol-then-and-over-the-rainbow-now.html, accessed November 23, 2015.

22 Stephen Holden, "Somewhere Over the Rainbow, Conjuring Judy Garland," *New York Times*, June 15, 2006, available online at http://www.nytimes.com/2006/06/15/arts/music/15judy.html, accessed January 15, 2017.

23 "Notes on the Program," *Playbill* for Carnegie Hall, June/July 2016.

24 Guy Trebay, "Rufus Wainwright Plays Judy Garland," *New York Times*, June 4, 2006, available online at http://www.nytimes.com/2006/06/04/fashion/sundaystyles/04RUFUS.html?n=Top/Reference/Times%20Topics/People/G/Garland,%20Judy, accessed November 28, 2015.

25 Dave Hughes, "Rufus Wainwright: Rufus Does Judy at Carnegie Hall," *Slant*, December 4, 2007, available online at http://www.slantmagazine.com/music/review/rufus-wainwright-rufus-does-judy-at-carnegie-hall, accessed November 28, 2015.

CHAPTER 5

1 The Jazz Discography Online, http://www.lordisco.com/tjd/CoverFrame, accessed April 21, 2017.

2 SecondHandSongs, https://secondhandsongs.com/performance/5316, accessed April 21, 2017.

3 https://secondhandsongs.com/statistics, accessed April 21, 2017.
4 Barbra Streisand, *One Voice*, Columbia, CK 40788.
5 *Carousel of American Music*, Music & Arts CD-971.
6 For a close analysis of Tatum's 1939 recording, with listening outline, see Scott DeVeaux and Gary Giddins, *Jazz*, 2nd ed. (New York: Norton, 2015), 216–17.
7 The overall form of Garner's "Over the Rainbow" can be represented as: Introduction–A–B–A–B–A–B–A–B–A–A–A–B–A–B–A–B–A–Coda (B/A).
8 Keith Jarrett, *La Scala*, ECM 1640, (1997), track 3.

CHAPTER 6

1 ABC Records 45-10982, October 1967.
2 *Billboard*, "World Digital Song Sales," http://www.billboard.com/biz/charts/world-digital-songs, accessed April 23, 2017.
3 On music, protest, and the Hawaiian Renaissance, see especially the writings of the sociologist George H. Lewis, including "Music, Culture, and the Hawaiian Renaissance," *Popular Music and Society* 10 (1986): 47–53, and "Style in Revolt: Music, Social Protest, and the Hawaiian Cultural Renaissance," *International Social Science Review* 62 (1987): 168–77.
4 Dan Kois, *Facing Future* (New York: Continuum, 2010), 7.
5 See Timothy D. Taylor, *Beyond Exoticism: Western Music and the World* (Durham, NC: Duke University Press, 2007), chapter 5.
6 Nate Chinen, "(Over the) Rainbow Warrior: Israel Kamakawiwo'ole and Another Kind of Somewhere," in *Pop When the World Falls Apart: Music in the Shadow of Doubt*, ed. Eric Weisbard (Durham, NC: Duke University Press, 2012), 178.
7 Kois, *Facing Future*, p. 68.
8 Louis Armstrong, "What a Wonderful World," on *Louis Armstrong and his Friends*, Amsterdam Records AMS-12009 (1970).
9 Chinen, "(Over the) Rainbow Warrior," 182. IZ's "Take Me Home Country Road" would have been modeled on the 1973 cover of the song by the reggae group Toots and the Maytals, who "Jamaica-ize" the lyrics in a similar manner. My thanks to Ben Saddock for making me aware of this connection.
10 See Amy Ku'uleailoha Stillman, "Textualizing Hawaiian Music," *American Music* 23 (2005): 69–94.
11 "Send a Little Aloha . . . in an 'Over the Rainbow' Musical Message Bottle!," April 19, 2013, http://www.izhawaii.com/send-a-little-aloha-in-an-over-the-rainbow-musical-message-bottle/, accessed July 12, 2016.
12 The official Israel Kamakawiwo'ole website lists videos in which his "Over the Rainbow" is featured. See http://www.izhawaii.com/milestones/, accessed August 29, 2016.

EPILOGUE

1 Linda Hansen, "Experiencing the World as Home: Reflections on Dorothy's Quest in 'The Wizard of Oz,'" *Soundings* 67 (1984): 96, 101.

2 Rushdie, *Wizard of Oz*, 24–25.

3 Available on YouTube at https://www.youtube.com/watch?v=k8XXfO5JQ48, accessed August 11, 2016.

4 Available on YouTube at https://www.youtube.com/watch?v=iMNtiSvQWyg, accessed June 6, 2017.

5 H. C. Baird, "R.A.F. Pilot Tells of Raid on Barges," *New York Times*, January 5, 1941, https://timesmachine.nytimes.com/timesmachine/1941/01/05/85248592.html?pageNumber=38, accessed January 27, 2017.

INDEX

www.ingramcontent.com/pod-product-compliance
Lightning Source LLC
LaVergne TN
LVHW010105170826
845678LV00012B/2254

9780190467340